Dear Family Member,

Many children think that math = difficulty. Scholastic's *100 Math Activities Kids Need to Do by 2nd Grade* will help your second grader realize that understanding + practice = math success.

Children need practice in order to develop mathematical thinking and mathematical skills. They need engaging examples in order to make abstract math ideas concrete. They need rich, varied opportunities in order to work successfully with math concepts and symbols. Your second grader will find all of that in our colorful, educational, *fun* activities.

The 100 activities in this workbook will help your child build his or her understanding of and facility with the key concepts and operations involved in

- number sense
- place value
- addition and subtraction
- multiplication and division
- fractions

- measurement
- geometry
- time
- money
- organizing data

A Math Skills list, on page 224, highlights the math skills in all of the activities in this workbook. These essential skills relate to the math curricula and standardized tests your child will be exposed to in school.

We've included a sheet of reusable math stickers, which your child can use to create number or word equations, solve number problems, and engage in all kinds of creative math play.

You are an important part of your child's math education, so we've also provided a few suggestions below for easily integrating math into your daily routine.

Scholastic's *100 Math Activities Kids Need to Do by 2nd Grade* will give your child math competence . . . and confidence. Enjoy!

Jean Feiwel
Scholastic Publisher, Senior Vice President

Parent Tips

- Read the directions on each activity page with your second grader. Make sure your child knows what to do. When he or she solves a problem, ask, "How do you know?" The more reasoning your child gives, the better.
- Put the math stickers where your child can easily see and reach them. Challenge your child to solve a new sticker equation each day.
- Play math games while you're driving, preparing meals, waiting in line, sitting in waiting rooms. They might include
  - saying two numbers and asking which one is greater than or less than the other
  - saying a four-digit number and asking which numeral is in the ones, tens, hundreds, or thousands place
  - posing simple addition or subtraction problems
  - asking multiplication riddles, such as "If 10 kids raised their hands, how many fingers would be in the air?"
  - playing "I spy" based on geometric shapes
- Use fractions and measurements while cooking with your child: "Give everyone one-fourth of the pizza." "Add 1 cup of milk."
- While grocery shopping, ask your child to compare products by size or price. Pick an item and ask what coin/bill combinations would add up to its price.
- Make a paper-plate clock with your child. Ask your child to show quarter and half hours on it at different hours. Write down analog or digital times and ask your child to show them on the clock.
- Help your child make a graph showing the daily weather for a month.

Editor: Sheila Keenan
Art Director: Nancy Sabato
Managing Editor: Karyn Browne
Production Editor: Bonnie Cutler
Project Management: Kevin Callahan, BNGO Books
Composition: Kevin Callahan, Patty Harris, Tony Lee, Daryl Richardson

Copyeditor/Proofreader: Geraldine Albert, Abigail Winograd
Cover: Red Herring Design
Editorial Consultant: Dale A. Beltzner, Jr., Elementary Math Specialist, Lower Milford Elementary School, Coopersburg, Pennsylvania
Activity Pages Writer: Katherine Burkett
Activity Pages Illustrator: Valeria Petrone

0-439-56680-0

12 11 10 9 8 7 6 5 4 3

13/0

Printed in the U.S.A.
First printing, May 2004

40

Photo Credits
Agefotostock 150 (school bus): Jack English.
Alamy 75 (motorcycle): National Motor Museum/Motoring Picture Library; 114: Andre Jenny; 115 (flashlight): Leslie Garland/LGPL; 219: GoodShoot.
Getty 24-25 (buttons): Photodisc; 94-95 (candy): Photodisc; 151 (ruler): Photodisc; 152 (milk carton): Foodpix; 152 (quart): Photodisc; 160 (ruler): Photodisc.
Photo Edit 6: David Young Wolf; 7: Mary Francis; 45 (both): Tony Freeman; 90 (dogs): Amy Etra; 103 (all): David Young Wolff; 154 (letter): Felicia Martinez; 158 (family): David Kelly Crow; 159 (surfing): David Young Wolff; 202 (calendar with cartoon): Tony Freeman.
PictureQuest 54: Creatas/Creatas; 62: Ryan McVay/Photodisc; 63: Creatas/Creatas; 74 (koala): Barry Peake/Rex Intstock/Stock Connection, (chocolate): Burke/Triolo/Brand X Pictures; 75 (saguaro cactus): Robert Glusic/Photodisc, (millipede): Burke/Triolo/Brand X Pictures; 76: IT Stock Free; 82: SuperStock/SuperStock; 84 (top): Rubberball Productions/Rubberball Productions; 85 (top): Rubberball Productions/ Rubberball Productions, (middle): Creatas/Creatas; 91 (starfish): Joe Atlas/Brand X Pictures, (skateboard): C Squared Studios/Photodisc; 99: C Squared Studios/Photodisc; 100-101 (starfish): Joe Atlas/Brand X Pictures; 115 (flashlight): F.Schussler/PhotoLink/Photodisc; 116 (top): Creatas/Creatas, (bottom): Rubberball Productions/Rubberball Productions; 117 (middle): Rubberball Productions/Rubberball Productions; 138: Creatas/Creatas; 139: Banana Stock/Banana Stock Ltd.; 148 (eraser): C Squared Studios/Photodisc, (crayon): C Squared Studios/Photodisc, (pink eraser): Joe Atlas/Brand X Pictures;

149 (notebook): Stockbyte, (tape dispenser): Joe Atlas/Brand X Pictures, (paper clip): Photodisc/Photodisc; 150 (child): Creatas/Creatas; 151 (pet mouse): Jim Corwin/Index Stock Imagery; 152 (measuring cup): Corbis Images, (gallon): Ryan McVay/Photodisc, (liter): ImageState-Pictor/ImageState-Pictor; 188 (selling lemonade): Keith Brofsky/Brand X Pictures; 202 (girl): SuperStock/SuperStock; 207(brown dog): G.K. & Vikki Hart/Photodisc.
SODA 18 (orange & banana): Photodisc via SODA; 19 (banana & apple): Photodisc via SODA, (watermelon): Peter Neumann via SODA; 44: David Waitz via SODA; 45 (girl): Francis Clark Westfield via SODA; 52 (apple): Photodisc via SODA, (girl): Francis Clark Westfield via SODA; 53 (orange): Photodisc via SODA; 84 (boy waving): Gerri Hernandez via SODA, (girl): David Mager via SODA; 85 (bottom): David Mager via SODA; 90 (children from left to right): Stanley Bach via SODA; Gerri Hernandez via SODA, Francis Clark Westfield via SODA, David Mager via SODA; 91 (rabbit & flowers & ladybug): Photodisc via SODA; 98: Photodisc via SODA; 112-113 (apple): Photodisc via SODA; 115 (sleeping bag): David Waitz via SODA; 116 (middle): David Mager via SODA; 117 (boy waving): Gerri Hernandez via SODA, (girl): David Mager via SODA; 148 (scissor): James Levin/Studio 10/SODA; 154 (guinea pig & elephant): Photodisc via SODA; 158 (girl): Image 100 Ltd. Via SODA; 159 (snowman): Richard Hutchings via SODA; 160 (thermometer): David Lawrence via SODA, (measuring cup): Scott Campbell via SODA; 190: John Fortunado via SODA; 191: David Mager via SODA; 202: (diary): Photodisc via SODA, (clock): Artville via SODA; 203: Stanley Bach via SODA; 207: (white dog & black and white dog) Photodisc via SODA; 218 (shells): John Lei via SODA.

Contents

Number Words

Write the matching number or number word.

__1__ one   20 twenty _____

7 _____   _____ ninety

thirteen _____   _____ one hundred

_____ eighteen   1,000 _____

Now write the number or number word that goes with
each fact below. Don't forget to use hyphens with two-digit
numbers from twenty-one to ninety-nine.

Number of bones in a baby's body:

300 _____

Number of bones in a grown-up's body:

_____ two hundred six

Number of muscles used in smiling:

_____ seventeen

Number of muscles used in frowning:

43 _____

Life span of a taste bud, in days: 10 _____

Number of ear glands that make wax:

2,000 _____

Number of cups of digestive juices your body makes each day:

thirty-two _____

Number of months it takes an adult's fingernail to grow one inch:

8 _____

Number of seconds a red blood cell takes to travel around your body:

20 _____

Number of days a red blood cell lives:

one hundred twenty _____

Number of inches a person's hair grows per year: 6 _____

Number of hairs a head loses each day:

45 _____

Number of breaths a person takes per hour:

960 _____

Number of skin particles shed each second:

One hundred sixty-seven _____

Number of colds a person catches in a lifetime:

250 _____

Number of people who can't tickle you:

1 _____ (Can you guess who?)

That's Great . . . er

> means "greater than": 6 > 5
< means "less than": 5 < 6
= means "is equal to": 6 = 6

Draw >, <, or = to tell about the number pair, word pair,
or number-and-word pair.

21 _____ 16   13 _____ 18

14 _____ 41   sixteen _____ sixty

thirty-three _____ 33   0 _____ 4

100 _____ 10   12 _____ 12

74 _____ 37   19 _____ 9

Answer each pair of questions.
Then compare your number answers using >, <, or =.

How many grown-ups in your family? _____

How many kids in your family? _____

_____

How many people live in your home? _____

How many pets live in your home? _____

_____

How many girl cousins do you have? _____

How many boy cousins do you have? _____

_____

How many people do you know
with the same first name as you?

_____

How many people do you know
with the same last name as you?

_____

_____

How many pairs of your shoes have shoelaces? _____

How many pairs of your shoes don't have shoelaces? _____

_____

How many doors are there in your home? _____

How many windows are there in your home? _____

_____

How many times can you hop on your right foot

without falling? _____

How many times can you hop on your left foot

without falling? _____

_____

Who's First?

Ordinal numbers tell about the order in a series.

Draw lines to match these ordinal numbers with their names.

first	10th
second	4th
third	8th
fourth	1st
fifth	5th
sixth	9th
seventh	2nd
eighth	6th
ninth	3rd
tenth	7th

8   **Number Sense & Place Value**

Write the correct ordinal number on each medal.

Write the correct ordinal number words next to each medal.

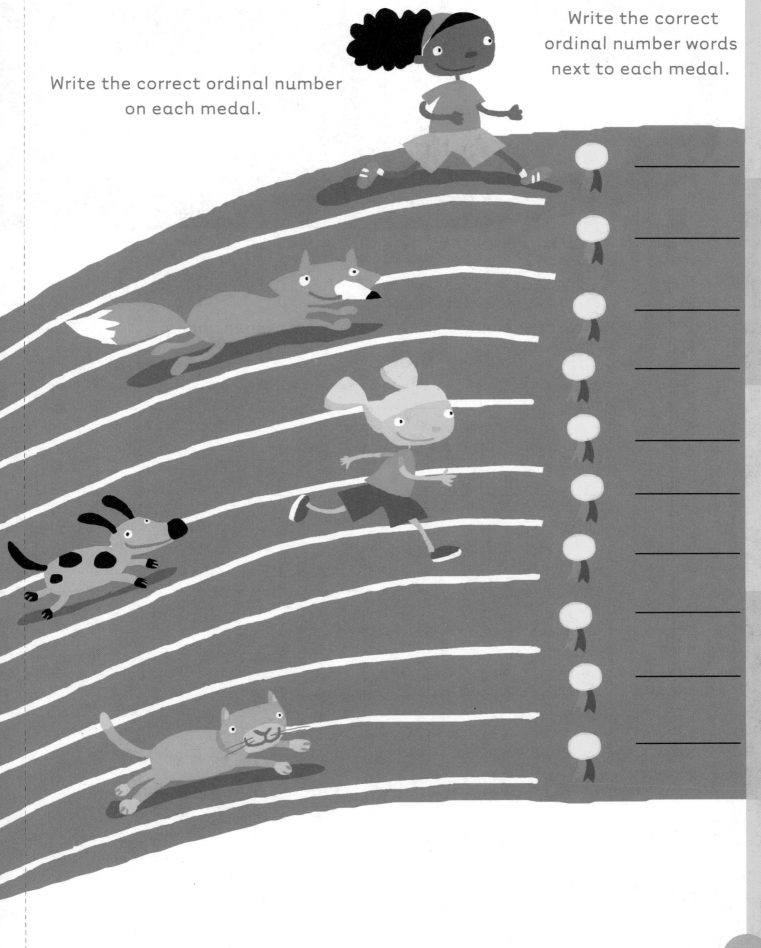

_____

_____

_____

_____

_____

_____

_____

_____

_____

_____

Count Your Chickens

Write the numbers that come next, counting up.

105 _____ _____ (t) _____ _____

76 (r) _____ _____ _____ _____

219 _____ _____ _____ _____

14 _____ _____ _____ (s)

57 _____ _____ _____ _____ _____

321 _____ _____ _____ (h) _____

Write the numbers that come before by counting backward.

36 _____ ⟨c⟩ _____ _____ _____

5 _____ _____ _____ _____ _____

228 _____ _____ _____ ⟨c⟩ _____

164 _____ _____ _____ _____ _____

100 ⟨a⟩ _____ _____ _____ _____

44 _____ _____ _____ _____ _____

Put the circled answers in number order. Then write
the letters below them to solve this riddle.

How do chickens start a race?

From _____ _____ _____ _____

Counting Review

Write the missing number in each series. Find the answer in the list on the right. Then cross out the ice cream flavor next to it. When you're finished, you'll have a list of the top five flavors.

33	_____	35	998	_____	1,000
20	_____	22	129	_____	131
156	_____	158	51	_____	53
410	_____	412	72	_____	74
7	_____	9	99	_____	101
14	_____	16	1,450	_____	1,452
690	_____	692	38	_____	40
79	_____	81	87	_____	89
259	_____	261	168	_____	170
45	_____	47	399	_____	401

1,451	chocolate chip	57	chocolate
999	coconut-pineapple	52	chocolate peanut-butter cup
691	spumoni	47	Neapolitan (vanilla, chocolate, and strawberry)
411	peach		
400	pralines & cream	46	strawberry
260	rum raisin	39	cookie dough
171	vanilla	34	cherry vanilla
169	bubble gum	25	butter pecan
130	rocky road	21	black walnut
157	peppermint	20	cookies & cream
100	mango	15	caramel swirl
88	banana fudge	8	coffee
80	maple nut		
73	mint chocolate chip		

Circle the top five ice cream flavors. The number next to those flavors tells how many millions of gallons are sold in the U.S. each year.

Skip Counting

First count by 1s. Then use skip counting by 2s, 5s, or 10s to see how many.

Count the puppy tails by 1s.

_____ _____ _____ _____

_____ _____ _____ _____

Count the rabbit ears by 2s.

_____ _____ _____ _____ _____

_____ _____ _____

Count the starfish arms by 5s.

_____ _____ _____ _____ _____

Count the butterfly spots by 10s.

_____ _____ _____ _____ _____

_____ _____ _____ _____

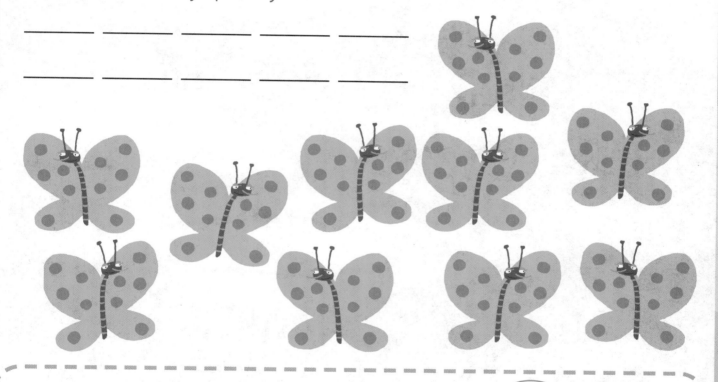

Use the number strip below to skip count by your age. (Circle) the number that matches your age. Then go to the next number, and count up using your age number. Circle the new number. Keep going until you run out of numbers on the strip.

1 2 3 4 5 6 7 8 9 10 11 12 13 14 15 16 17 18 19 20 21 22 23 24

25 26 27 28 29 30 31 32 33 34 35 36 37 38 39 40 41 42 43 44 45

46 47 48 49 50 51 52 53 54 55 56 57 58 59 60 61 62 63 64 65 66

Insect Estimates

Estimate, or tell about how many, insects there are in each group. Then count to check your answer.

Circle the best estimate:

5 10 20 50

Now count the bees.

How many are there? _____

Circle the best estimate:

5 10 20 50

Now count the grasshoppers.

How many are there? _____

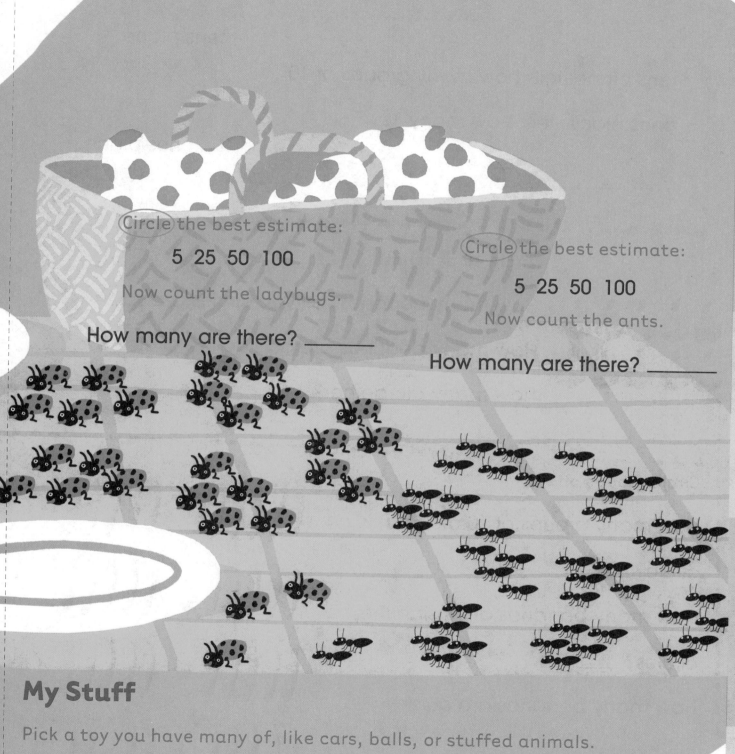

Circle the best estimate:

5 25 50 100

Now count the ladybugs.

How many are there? _____

Circle the best estimate:

5 25 50 100

Now count the ants.

How many are there? _____

My Stuff

Pick a toy you have many of, like cars, balls, or stuffed animals.

Estimate how many you have: _____

Now count the toys.

How many are there? _____

Fruit by the Bunch

tens place: tells how many groups of 10

ones place: tells how many 1s

tens place

↓

1 5

↑

ones place

Circle 10 peaches.

How many peaches did you circle? _____

How many peaches are outside the circle? _____

How many altogether? _____

Circle groups of 10.

How many groups of 10 did you

circle? _____

How many bananas are inside the

circles? _____

How many bananas are outside

the circles? _____

How many altogether? _____

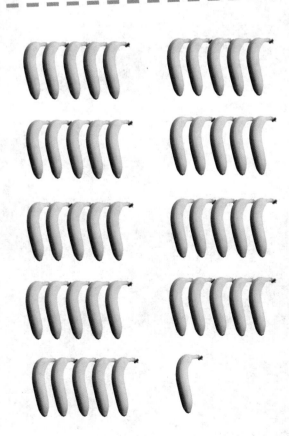

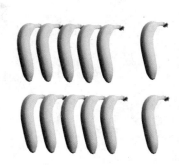

How many bananas did you circle? _____

How many bananas are outside the circle? _____

How many altogether? _____

Circle groups of 10.

How many groups of 10 did you circle?

_____

How many apples are inside the circles?

_____

How many apples are outside the circles?

_____

How many altogether? _____

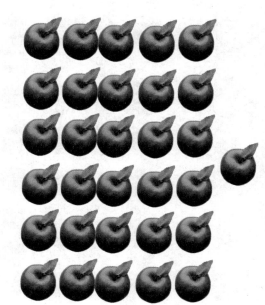

Circle groups of 10.

How many groups of 10 did you circle? _____

How many slices of watermelon are inside

the circles? _____

How many slices are outside the circles?

_____

How many altogether? _____

Bubbling Up

How many bubbles in each group?
Fill in the green bubble next to the correct number.

z ◯ 57
r ◯ 65
b ◯ 78
l ◯ 77

a ◯ 10
n ◯ 20
i ◯ 30
e ◯ 40

s ◯ 25
o ◯ 26
e ◯ 52
x ◯ 62

q ◯ 10
m ◯ 13
i ◯ 18
f ◯ 81

t ◯ 10
d ◯ 13
w ◯ 31
a ◯ 33

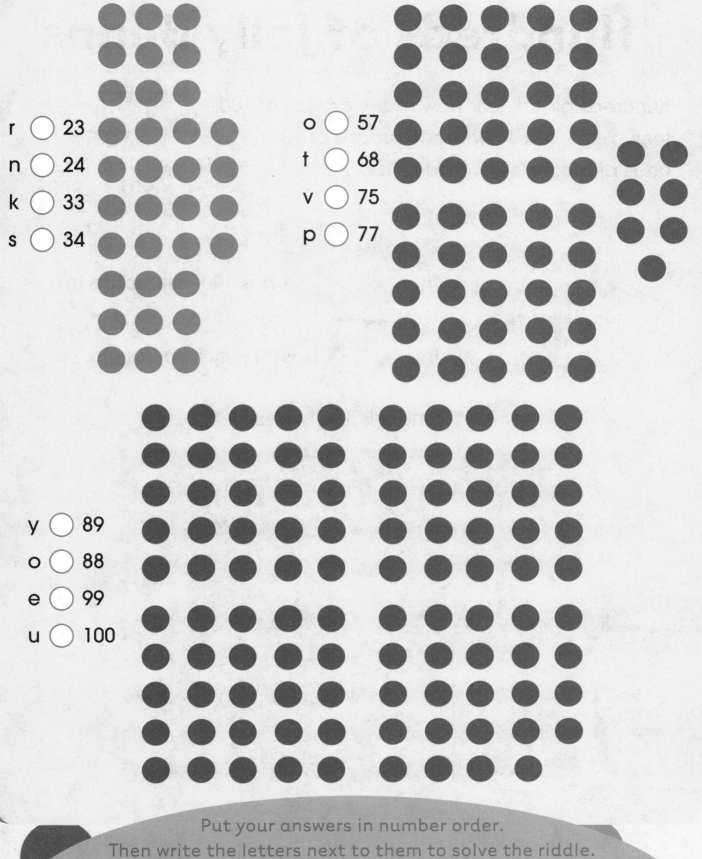

r ◯ 23
n ◯ 24
k ◯ 33
s ◯ 34

o ◯ 57
t ◯ 68
v ◯ 75
p ◯ 77

y ◯ 89
o ◯ 88
e ◯ 99
u ◯ 100

Put your answers in number order.
Then write the letters next to them to solve the riddle.

What do you call a T. Rex that stubbed its toe?

A _____-_____

Hundreds of Jelly Beans

hundreds place: tells how many groups of 100

tens place: tells how many groups of 10

ones place: tells how many 1s

hundreds

3 2 5

tens   ones

Look at the pictures. Write how many jelly beans there are altogether.

This has 100 jelly beans in it.

This has 10 jelly beans in it.

This  is 1 jelly bean.

_____

_____

_____

_____

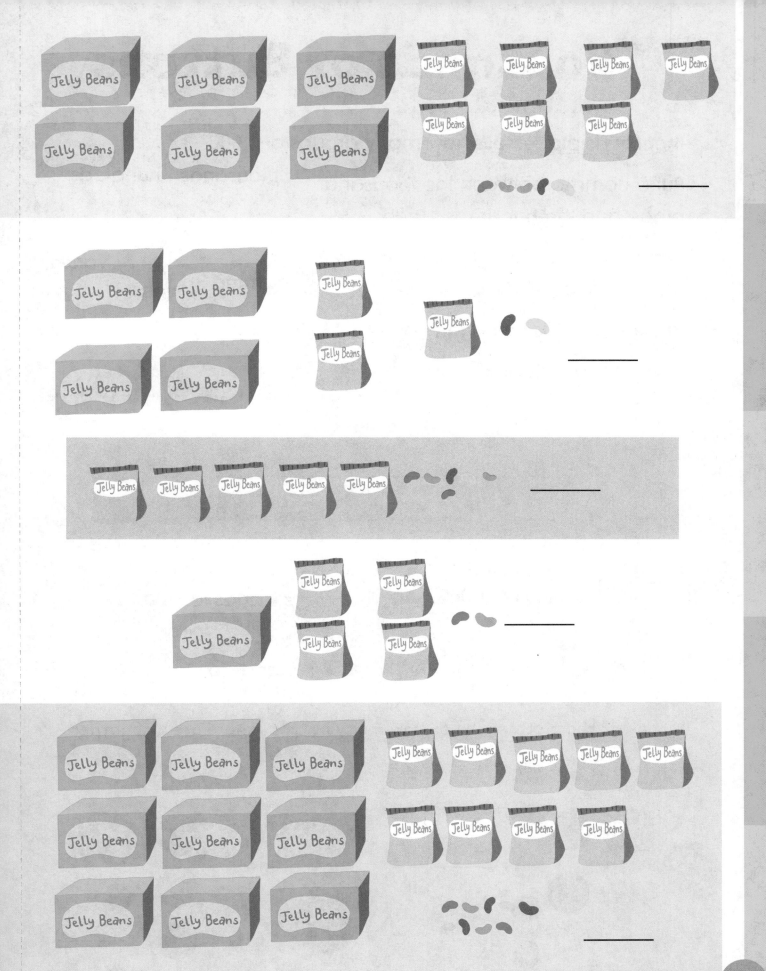

Thousands of Buttons

thousands place: tells how many groups of 1,000

Put a comma between the thousands place and the hundreds place.

hundreds place: tells how many groups of 100

tens place: tells how many groups of 10

ones place: tells how many 1s

1,325

thousands   hundreds   comma   tens   ones

First skip count by 100s.

100 _____ _____ _____ _____

_____ _____ _____ _____ 1,000

This ⬤ stands for 1,000.   This ⬤ stands for 100.

This ⬤ stands for 10.   This ⬤ stands for 1.

Look at the pictures. Write how many buttons there are altogether.

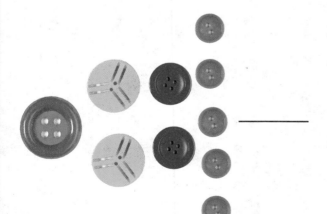

_____

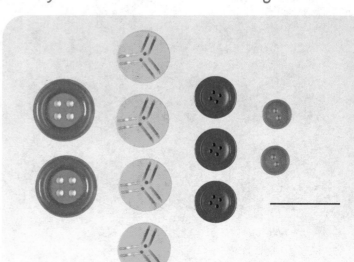

_____

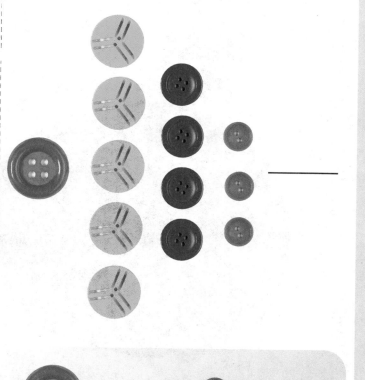

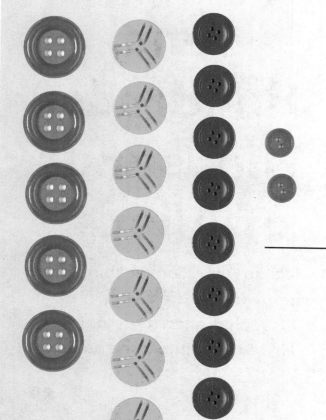

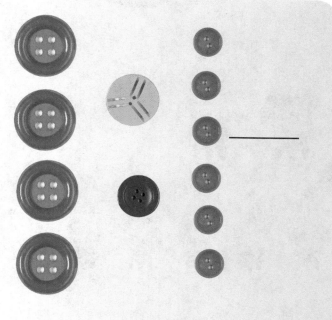

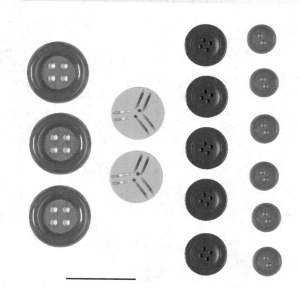

Circle the correct answer.

Which number has 7 thousands?
7,865   8,765   6,578

Which number has 9 tens?
297   9,789   1,239

Which number has 6 ones?
4,662   426   2,605

Which number has 3 hundreds?
2,943   6,538   9,307

Tens, Hundreds, Thousands of Aliens!

It's an Alien Convention! How many aliens are flying in from each planet to attend? Write the number in the box.

Planet Shushaz

[ ] attending

Planet Drax

[ ] attending

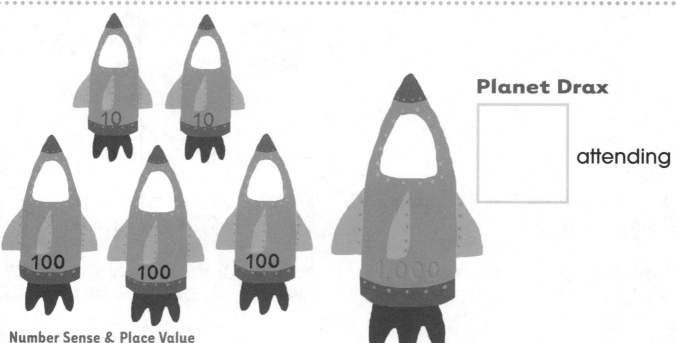

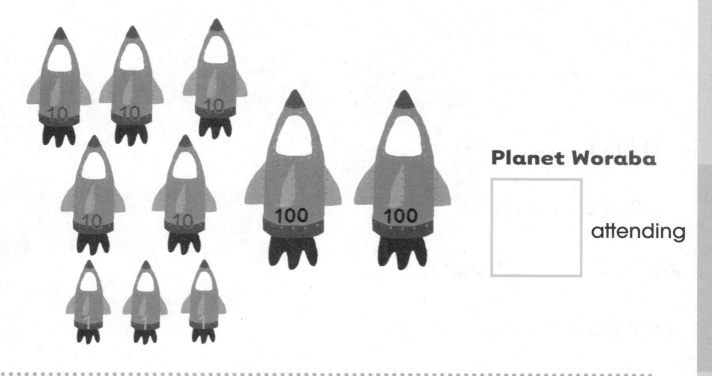

Planet Woraba

☐ attending

Planet Zeebor ☐ attending

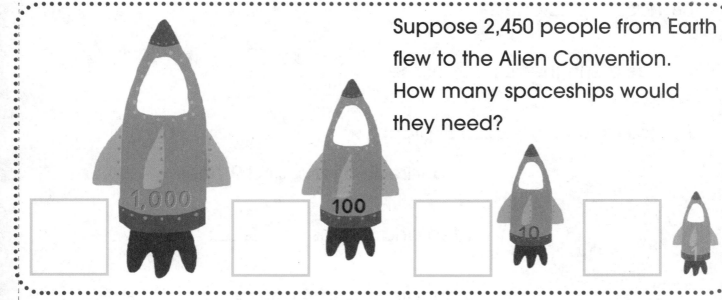

Suppose 2,450 people from Earth flew to the Alien Convention. How many spaceships would they need?

Placing Place Value

Solve each problem. Find the answers on the blue lines in the picture.
Color those sections blue to find the answer to the
science question on page 29.

119 has _____ ones.

452 has _____ tens.

2,510 has _____ thousands.

662 has a 2 in the _____ place.

341 has _____ hundreds.

748 has a 7 in the _____ place.

875 has _____ tens.

4,003 has _____ hundreds.

64 has _____ tens.

58 has _____ ones.

2,344 has a 2 in the _____ place.

1,583 has an 8 in the _____ place.

7 hundreds, 5 tens, and 9 ones = _____.

1 ten and 3 ones = _____.

5 hundreds and 4 ones = _____.

1 thousand and 6 tens = _____.

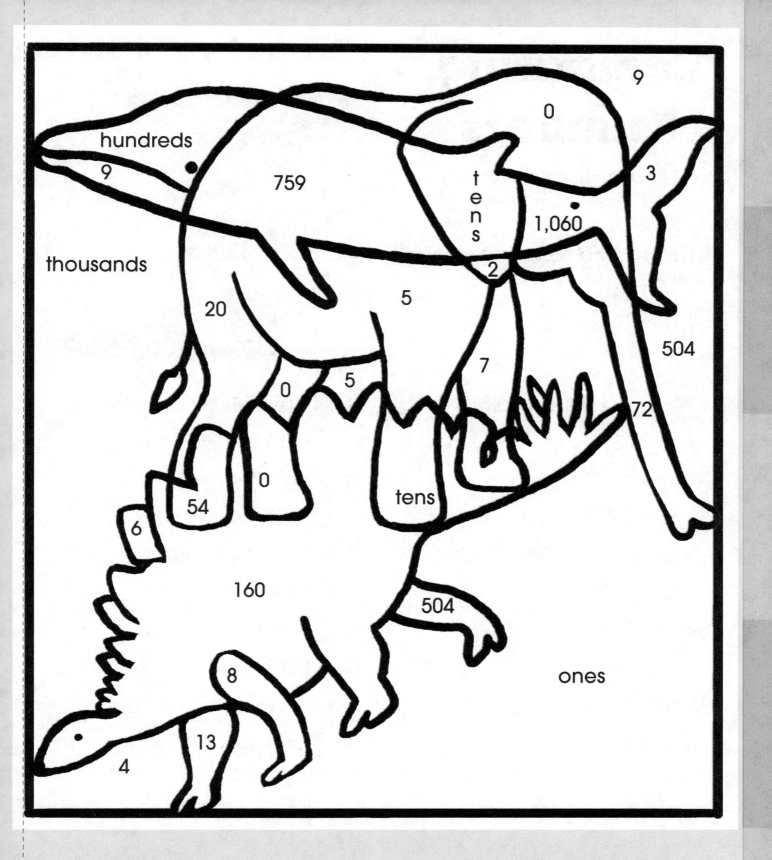

Which is the largest animal that ever lived: an African elephant, a blue whale, or a Supersaurus dinosaur?

_____

Comparing Numbers

Fill in the bubble next to the correct answer.

Which is the greatest number?

t ○ 64

r ○ 640

m ○ 6

Which is the least number?

r ○ 382

l ○ 14

b ○ 1,024

Which is the greatest number?

u ○ 250

e ○ 350

i ○ 150

Which is the least number?

o ○ 444

p ○ 544

i ○ 711

Which is the least number?

e ○ 789

g ○ 622

o ○ 515

Which is the greatest number?

v ○ 752

t ○ 792

d ○ 782

Which is the least number?

t ○ 641

o ○ 683

u ○ 614

Which is the greatest number?

i ◯ 1,450

a ◯ 1,875

o ◯ 1,399

Which is the greatest number?

l ◯ 356

h ◯ 339

r ◯ 358

Which is the greatest number?

c ◯ 3,389

n ◯ 3,349

y ◯ 3,329

Which is the least number?

b ◯ 399

c ◯ 392

m ◯ 395

Which is the greatest number?

t ◯ 2,226

r ◯ 2,228

w ◯ 2,239

Find the answer that matches each number below. Write the letter next to that answer on the lines below to solve the riddle.

What did the cowgirl use to count her herd?

H ___ ___
    350 640

___ ___ ___ ___ ___ ___ ___ ___ ___ ___
3,389 515 2,239 392 614 14 1,875 792 444 358

Hundreds Chart

Follow the directions to fill in the number chart.

Number Sense & Place Value

Write in the numbers between 1 and 10. (Go straight across.)
What did you count by? Circle your answer.

1s 2s 5s 10s

Write in the numbers between 10 and 100.
(Go straight down.)
What did you count by? Circle your answer.

1s 2s 5s 10s

Write in the numbers from 61 to 69.
Write in the numbers from 11 to 19.
Write in the numbers between 35 and 39.
Write in the numbers in the two empty boxes below 37.
Write in the numbers from 91 to 99.
Write in the numbers in all the empty boxes below 8.
Write in the missing numbers from 21 to 34.
Write in the missing numbers from 41 to 89.

Place-Value Game

You'll need a partner; the hundreds chart on page 32 as the game board; 2 markers (for example, different buttons or beans), one for each player; 1 dime and 1 penny.

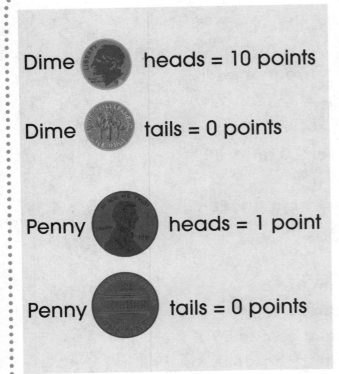

Dime heads = 10 points

Dime tails = 0 points

Penny heads = 1 point

Penny tails = 0 points

Which way do you move your marker if the penny lands on heads? Hint: How do you add 1 on the hundreds chart?

Which way do you move your marker if the dime lands on heads? Hint: How do you add 10 on the hundreds chart?

What do you do if both coins land on heads?

What do you do if both coins land on tails?

Rule: A player must get at least one head to put a marker on the board.

1. The younger player goes first and flips both coins. To figure out the points, look at the list. The first player puts a marker on the number that matches the score.
2. The second player flips both coins and puts a marker on the board that matches the score.
3. Keep taking turns until one player reaches 100. (You don't have to land exactly on it.)

Number Sense & Place Value Answer Key

Note: Answers read across, per page.

4–5 seven, 90, 13, 100, 18, one thousand; three hundred, 206, 17, forty-three, ten, two thousand, 32, eight, twenty, 120, six, forty-five, nine hundred sixty, 167, two hundred fifty, one

6–7 >, <, <, <, =, <, >, =, >, >; answers will vary.

8–9 first/1st, second/2nd, third/3rd, fourth/4th, fifth/5th, sixth/6th, seventh/7th, eighth/8th; ninth/9th; tenth/10th; 1st/first, 10th/tenth, 3rd/third, 6th/sixth, 8th/eighth, 5th/fifth, 2nd/second, 7th/seventh, 9th/ninth, 4th/fourth

10–11 106, 107, 108, 109, 110; 77, 78, 79, 80, 81; 220, 221, 222, 223, 224; 15, 16, 17, 18, 19; 58, 59, 60, 61, 62; 322, 323, 324, 325, 326; 35, 34, 33, 32, 31; 4, 3, 2, 1, 0; 227, 226, 225, 224, 223; 163, 162, 161, 160, 159; 99, 98, 97, 96, 95; 43, 42, 41, 40, 39; scratch

12–13 34, 999, 21, 130, 157, 52, 411, 73, 8, 100, 15, 1,451, 691, 39, 80, 88, 260, 169, 46, 400; vanilla, chocolate, Neapolitan, butter pecan, cookies & cream

14–15 1, 2, 3, 4, 5, 6, 7, 8, 9, 10; 2, 4, 6, 8, 10, 12, 14, 16, 18, 20; 5, 10, 15, 20, 25; 10, 20, 30, 40, 50, 60, 70, 80, 90, 100; answers will vary.

16–17 10, 11; 5, 6; 25, 28; 50, 47; answers will vary.

18–19 10, 0, 10; 4, 40, 6, 46; 10, 2, 12; 3, 30, 1, 31; 2, 20, 0, 20

20–21 65, 20, 26, 18, 13, 34, 57, 99; dino-sore

22–23 112, 517, 233, 827, 675, 432, 56, 142, 999

24–25 200, 300, 400, 500, 600, 700, 800, 900; 1,225, 2,432, 1,543, 5,782, 4,116, 3,256; 7,865, 426, 297, 9,307

26–27 Shushaz/1,025, Drax /1,320, Woraba /253, Zeebor/102; 2, 4, 5, 0

28–29 9, 5, 2, ones, 3, hundreds, 7, 0, 6, 8, thousands, tens, 759, 13, 504, 1,060; coloring reveals blue whale.

30–31 640, 14, 515, 350, 792, 444, 614, 1,875, 358, 3,389, 392, 2,239; Her cowculator

32–33 1s, 10s; number chart completed with numbers from 1 to 100

Animal Equations

Write an equation like the one below for each set of pictures.

3 + 2 = 5

_____

_____

_____

_____

How many equal signs (=) did you need to write the equations above?

n ◯ 1   l ◯ 4   r ◯ 8

• •

Circle the equations that **equal 10**.

5 + 5	9 − 1	10 + 0	9 + 0
7 + 2	8 + 2	4 + 6	7 + 4
8 + 5	13 + 3	8 + 5	3 + 7
11 − 1	14 − 4	9 + 1	0 + 10
7 + 3	1 + 9	2 + 8	6 + 4

How many equations did you circle?

i ◯ 11   o ◯ 12   e ◯ 13

Fill in the missing parts of these equations.

$2 \underline{\hspace{1cm}} 3 = 5$

$7 - 7 = \underline{\hspace{1cm}}$

$6 - 5 = \underline{\hspace{1cm}}$

$8 \underline{\hspace{1cm}} 2 = 6$

$9 + 5 = \underline{\hspace{1cm}}$

$14 \underline{\hspace{1cm}} 10 = 4$

$11 - 1 = \underline{\hspace{1cm}}$

$\underline{\hspace{1cm}} - 2 = 6$

$1 + \underline{\hspace{1cm}} = 5$

$4 + \underline{\hspace{1cm}} = 11$

How many of your answers were minus signs (—)?

m ◯ 1   t ◯ 2   d ◯ 3

Cross out the extra number in each equation.

$2 + 4 + 3 = 6$

$6 + 0 + 2 = 2$

$7 + 6 + 6 = 13$

$7 + 8 + 8 = 16$

$1 + 3 + 4 = 5$

$8 + 7 + 8 = 16$

$9 + 8 + 10 = 17$

$2 + 9 + 8 = 11$

$10 + 5 + 4 = 15$

$3 + 7 + 9 = 12$

How many 7s did you cross out?

p ◯ 2   b ◯ 3   f ◯ 4

Use the letters next to your answers to solve the riddle.

What did the zero say to the eight?

Nice $\underline{\hspace{1cm}}$ $\underline{\hspace{1cm}}$ $\underline{\hspace{1cm}}$ $\underline{\hspace{1cm}}$!

3   13   4   2

Sum Fun

Adding is putting things together. The **plus** sign (+) tells you to add. The answer you get is called a **sum**.

Add. Write the sum on the line.

$4 + 5 =$ _____

$8 + 8 =$ _____

$10 + 4 =$ _____

$3 + 9 =$ _____

$9 + 2 =$ _____

When you're adding numbers, it doesn't matter which one comes first. The sum will be the same. This is called the **commutative property** of addition.

$4 + 3 = 7$
•••• ••• •••••••

$3 + 4 = 7$
••• •••• •••••••

Fill in the missing numbers.

2 + 3 = 5

_____ + 2 = 5

7 + 1 = 8

_____ + 7 = 8

_____ + 5 = 9

5 + 4 = 9

7 + 3 = 10

3 + _____ = 10

Now it's your turn. Write two equations for each sum.

_____ + _____ = 7

_____ + _____ = 7

_____ + _____ = 12

_____ + _____ = 12

_____ + _____ = 16

_____ + _____ = 16

What's the Difference?

Subtraction is taking things away. The **minus sign** (−) tells you to subtract. The answer you get is the **difference**.

Subtract. Write the difference below the lines.

$$6 - 1$$

$$8 - 4$$

$$10 - 9$$

$$5 - 3$$

$$6 - 0$$

$$11 - 8$$

If you know this number fact—

$$8 + 1 = 9$$

—then you also know these number facts:

$$9 - 8 = 1$$

and

$$9 - 1 = 8$$

These three equations are in the same number-fact family.

Fill in the missing numbers and signs. Then draw lines
to match the related number facts.

4 + 3 = _____

12 − 7 = _____

14 − _____ = 8

5 + 7 = _____

11 _____ 2 = 9

_____ − 3 = 4

10 + _____ = 10

10 − _____ = 0

_____ − 5 = 7

11 − _____ = 2

2 + 9 = 11

7 − _____ = 3

_____ − 8 = 6

_____ + 8 = 14

10 − 0 = _____

Add, Add, Add!

Add two numbers first. Then add the third number.

Hint: Look for combinations of 10.

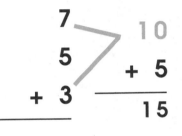

```
  4
  2  →  6
+ 7    + 7
____   ____
        13
```

```
  7
  5  →  10
+ 3    + 5
____   ____
        15
```

Add these numbers. Show how you broke each one down into smaller equations. (Note: Some equations have letters next to them.)

```
    1        7        3        5        2
    2        8        3        6        4
  + 1      + 2      + 1      + 5      + 2
  _____    _____    _____    _____    _____
     r                  i                  a
```

```
    2        3        3        5        9
    4        5        3        2        1
  + 8      + 2      + 7      + 2      + 2
  _____    _____    _____    _____    _____
              h                  a
```

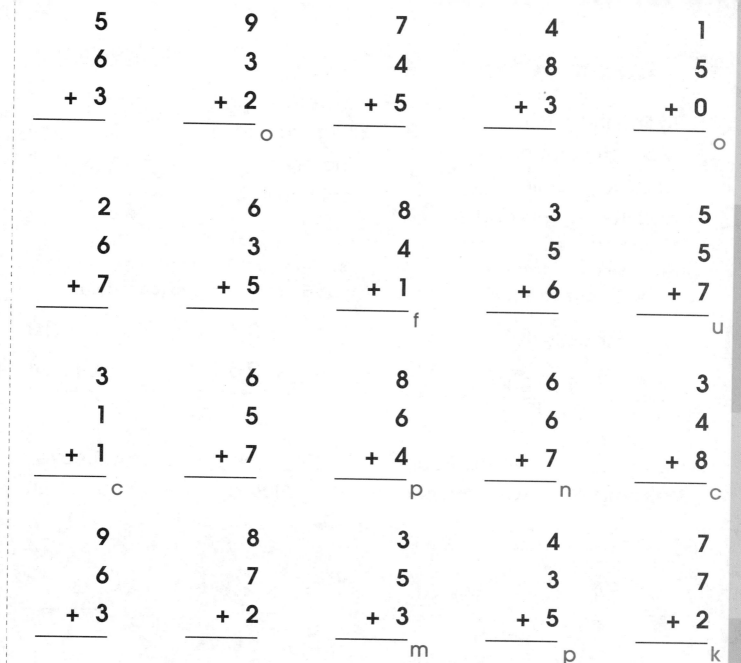

5	9	7	4	1
6	3	4	8	5
+ 3	+ 2	+ 5	+ 3	+ 0
	o			o

2	6	8	3	5
6	3	4	5	5
+ 7	+ 5	+ 1	+ 6	+ 7
		f		u

3	6	8	6	3
1	5	6	6	4
+ 1	+ 7	+ 4	+ 7	+ 8
c		p	n	c

9	8	3	4	7
6	7	5	3	7
+ 3	+ 2	+ 3	+ 5	+ 2
		m	p	k

Find the sum that matches each number below. Write the letters next to those sums on the lines below to solve the riddle.

Why was Cinderella a terrible basketball player?

Because she had a ____ ____ ____ ____ ____ ____ ____
12   17   11   18   16   7   19

____ ____ ____ ____ ____ ____ ____ ____ ____ !
13   14   4   9   5   6   8   15   10

Nonsense Names . . . or Not?

To find the **sum** of two-digit numbers, add the **ones** first and the **tens** second.

$$\begin{array}{r} 13 \\ + 22 \\ \hline 35 \end{array}$$

Hint: Line up the **ones** column first.

$$\begin{array}{r} 42 \\ + 4 \\ \hline 46 \end{array}$$

Are these city names for real? Add these numbers. Then check their sums in the box to see if the silly city name below the equation is real.

$$\begin{array}{r} 12 \\ + 24 \\ \hline \end{array}$$

$$\begin{array}{r} 20 \\ + 14 \\ \hline \end{array}$$

$$\begin{array}{r} 33 \\ + 25 \\ \hline \end{array}$$

$$\begin{array}{r} 20 \\ + 4 \\ \hline \end{array}$$

Muck City, Alabama

Teddy Bear, West Virginia

Eek, Alaska

Jaw Breaker, Utah

$$\begin{array}{r} 45 \\ + 54 \\ \hline \end{array}$$

$$\begin{array}{r} 17 \\ + 60 \\ \hline \end{array}$$

$$\begin{array}{r} 37 \\ + 22 \\ \hline \end{array}$$

$$\begin{array}{r} 94 \\ + 3 \\ \hline \end{array}$$

Bummerville, California

Pitchfork Junction, North Dakota

Cry Uncle, Indiana

Boring, Maryland

$$\begin{array}{r} 61 \\ + 32 \\ \hline \end{array}$$

$$\begin{array}{r} 40 \\ + 48 \\ \hline \end{array}$$

$$\begin{array}{r} 24 \\ + 45 \\ \hline \end{array}$$

$$\begin{array}{r} 32 \\ + 12 \\ \hline \end{array}$$

Tightsqueeze, Virginia

Frankenstein, Missouri

Scaredy Cat, Rhode Island

Belcher, New York

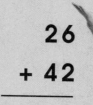

```
  71          48          26          17
+ 24        + 31        + 42        + 40
————        ————        ————        ————
```

Mickey
Moose,
Maine

Puddle Town,
Connecticut

Worstville,
Ohio

Sing Song,
Delaware

```
  31          81          56          43
+ 11        +  8        + 31        + 41
————        ————        ————        ————
```

Quiggleville,
Pennsylvania

Doghouse,
Nebraska

Frog Jump,
Tennessee

Nothingville,
Idaho

```
  66          23          43          22
+ 30        + 55        + 23        + 51
————        ————        ————        ————
```

Zzyzx,
California

Featherbird,
Georgia

Chump Change,
Louisiana

Nameless,
Tennessee

Real Names
36, 42, 44, 58, 68, 73, 79, 87,
88, 93, 96, 97, 99

Nonsense Names
24, 34, 39, 54, 57, 59,
66, 69, 77, 78, 84,
89, 95

```
  32          31
+ 22        +  8
————        ————
```

Wet Blanket,
Oregon

Diaper Rash,
Idaho

Good-Luck Charms

To find the **difference** between two-digit numbers, subtract the **ones** first and the tens second.

$$\begin{array}{r} 67 \\ -\ 22 \\ \hline 45 \end{array}$$

Hint: Line up the **ones** column first.

$$\begin{array}{r} 58 \\ -\ 4 \\ \hline 54 \end{array}$$

Subtract these numbers. Then check the differences in the box to see which of these things are considered lucky.

$$\begin{array}{r} 41 \\ -\ 20 \\ \hline \end{array}$$

Eating figs for breakfast on your birthday

$$\begin{array}{r} 66 \\ -\ 3 \\ \hline \end{array}$$

Pointing your thumbs up as you walk by a graveyard

$$\begin{array}{r} 87 \\ -\ 42 \\ \hline \end{array}$$

Sticking out your tongue when you walk into your bedroom

$$\begin{array}{r} 77 \\ -\ 34 \\ \hline \end{array}$$

Having a wad of gum stuck to your hat during a baseball game

$$\begin{array}{r} 95 \\ -\ 45 \\ \hline \end{array}$$

Accidentally putting on clothing inside out

$$\begin{array}{r} 68 \\ -\ 41 \\ \hline \end{array}$$

Tapping the goalie's shin pads before your hockey game

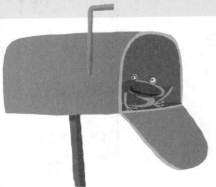

$$\begin{array}{r} 69 \\ -\ 54 \\ \hline \end{array}$$

Finding a toad in your mailbox

$$\begin{array}{r} 23 \\ -\ 11 \\ \hline \end{array}$$

Having a name with 7 letters

95
− 22
‾‾‾‾

Accidentally putting your mittens on your ears

52
− 41
‾‾‾‾

Sniffing your golf clubs before a game

98
− 23
‾‾‾‾

Finding white hair on a black cat

86
− 15
‾‾‾‾

Finding white hair in your grandfather's ears

58
− 35
‾‾‾‾

Eating an apple dipped in honey on New Year's Day

74
− 60
‾‾‾‾

Finding a stone with a hole in it

47
− 7
‾‾‾‾

Finding a sock with a hole in it

46
− 21
‾‾‾‾

Stepping on a grape

88
− 23
‾‾‾‾

Saying "rabbit, rabbit" first thing on the first day of each month

76
− 32
‾‾‾‾

Eating okra for dessert on your birthday

Somebody somewhere believes in the good-luck charms next to these differences:
12, 14, 21, 23, 27, 43, 63, 65, 73, 75

We made up the good-luck charms next to these differences:
11, 15, 25, 40, 44, 45, 50, 71

Sum, Sum, Sum Fun!

To find the sum of three-digit numbers, add the **ones** first, the **tens** second, and the **hundreds** third.

Hint: Line up the **ones** column first.

$$312 + 422 = 734$$

$$820 + 14 = 834$$

$$311 + 5 = 316$$

Add these numbers.

171 + 203	830 + 44	236 + 432	929 + 60	491 + 107	347 + 241
Boy,	you	shouldn't	help	yourself	pages
515 + 153	421 + 150	662 + 115	746 + 22	123 + 872	51 + 840
Wow!	sure	have	of	to	my

704	167	350	218	542	708
+ 212	+ 331	+ 626	+ 460	+ 231	+ 71
wish	you	a lot	of	problems,	don't

527	453	842	623	601	831
+ 132	+ 312	+ 103	+ 261	+ 207	+ 146
wouldn't	press	your	luck	says	you!

Circle the sums that have a 7 in the tens place.
Read the words below the circles to answer this riddle.

What did the spelling book say to the math book?

Keep On Subtracting!

To find the difference between three-digit numbers, subtract the **ones** first, the **tens** second, and the **hundreds** third.

$$\begin{array}{r} 655 \\ -\ 122 \\ \hline 533 \end{array}$$

Line up the **ones** column first. Treat an empty **hundreds** place as a 0.

$$\begin{array}{r} 758 \\ -\ 054 \\ \hline 704 \end{array}$$

Hint: If your answer has a 0 in the **ones** or **tens** place, be sure to include it in the difference.

$$\begin{array}{r} 245 \\ -\ 145 \\ \hline 100 \end{array}$$

Subtract. Find the differences.

678	934	719	297	378	357
− 456	− 411	− 405	− 287	− 155	− 155
Because	the	other	letters	paper	it

499	521	976	782	865	173
- 347	- 411	- 744	- 661	- 763	- 41
makes	water	the	numbers	oil	boil

945	999	792	297	378	507
- 530	- 437	- 760	- 296	- 164	- 105
its	and	the	the	flames	urn

763	234	646	499	524	495
- 320	- 112	- 213	- 222	- 223	- 471
were	burn	question	higher	jealous	reasons

Circle the differences that have a 2 in the ones place.
Read the words below the circles to answer this riddle.

Why is B such a hot letter?

Regroup and Add

Sometimes when you add, you need to regroup to find the sum easily. Here's how regrouping works.

1. Add the ones column.

$$\begin{array}{r} 4\,3 \\ +\ 2\,9 \\ \hline \end{array}$$

2. If the sum is higher than 9, regroup the number, and write it like this.

$$\begin{array}{r} {}^{1}\ \\ 4\,3 \\ +\ 2\,9 \\ \hline 2 \end{array}$$

3. Now add the tens column. Don't forget that the 1 really stands for one ten (12 = 1 ten + 2 ones), so it is added to the 40 + 20 already in the tens column. Include the number you regrouped from the ones column.

$$\begin{array}{r} {}^{1}\ \\ 4\,3 \\ +\ 2\,9 \\ \hline 7\,2 \end{array}$$

Add these numbers using regrouping.

$$\begin{array}{r} 27 \\ +\ 15 \\ \hline \end{array}\ \text{l} \qquad \begin{array}{r} 68 \\ +\ 27 \\ \hline \end{array}\ \text{i} \qquad \begin{array}{r} 11 \\ +\ 39 \\ \hline \end{array}\ \text{n} \qquad \begin{array}{r} 36 \\ +\ 45 \\ \hline \end{array}\ \text{o}$$

$$\begin{array}{r} 28 \\ +\ 48 \\ \hline \end{array}\ \text{i} \qquad \begin{array}{r} 49 \\ +\ 24 \\ \hline \end{array}\ \text{a} \qquad \begin{array}{r} 37 \\ +\ 16 \\ \hline \end{array}\ \text{r} \qquad \begin{array}{r} 35 \\ +\ 29 \\ \hline \end{array}\ \text{s}$$

$$
\begin{array}{r} 87 \\ +\ 9 \\ \hline \end{array}
$$
r

$$
\begin{array}{r} 46 \\ +28 \\ \hline \end{array}
$$
g

$$
\begin{array}{r} 27 \\ +34 \\ \hline \end{array}
$$
a

$$
\begin{array}{r} 56 \\ +26 \\ \hline \end{array}
$$
p

$$
\begin{array}{r} 49 \\ +26 \\ \hline \end{array}
$$
y

$$
\begin{array}{r} 65 \\ +15 \\ \hline \end{array}
$$
l

$$
\begin{array}{r} 87 \\ +\ 4 \\ \hline \end{array}
$$
f

$$
\begin{array}{r} 11 \\ +19 \\ \hline \end{array}
$$
a

$$
\begin{array}{r} 48 \\ +\ 3 \\ \hline \end{array}
$$
e

$$
\begin{array}{r} 46 \\ +24 \\ \hline \end{array}
$$
b

$$
\begin{array}{r} 19 \\ +35 \\ \hline \end{array}
$$
d

$$
\begin{array}{r} 52 \\ +19 \\ \hline \end{array}
$$
h

Find the sum that matches each number below. Write the letters next to those sums on the lines below to solve this riddle.

If you have 19 oranges in one hand and 25 apples in the other, what do you have?

A ___ ___ ___ ___ ___ ___
  96   51   73   42   80   75

___ ___ ___   ___ ___ ___ ___
  70   95   74   82   30   76   53

___ ___   ___ ___ ___ ___ ___!
  81   91   71   61   50   54   64

More Regrouping

Add these numbers using regrouping.

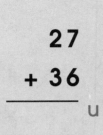

```
  27
+ 36
————
      u
```

```
  17
+ 16
————
      g
```

```
  49
+ 13
————
      a
```

```
  86
+  7
————
      r
```

```
  62
+ 28
————
      l
```

```
  54
+ 17
————
      e
```

```
  46
+  5
————
      t
```

```
  38
+ 38
————
      i
```

$$\begin{array}{r} 77 \\ + 18 \\ \hline \end{array}$$ o

$$\begin{array}{r} 34 \\ + 47 \\ \hline \end{array}$$ p

$$\begin{array}{r} 19 \\ + 53 \\ \hline \end{array}$$ t

$$\begin{array}{r} 27 \\ + 25 \\ \hline \end{array}$$ y

$$\begin{array}{r} 61 \\ + 19 \\ \hline \end{array}$$ h

$$\begin{array}{r} 11 \\ + 39 \\ \hline \end{array}$$ n

$$\begin{array}{r} 15 \\ + 27 \\ \hline \end{array}$$ e

$$\begin{array}{r} 36 \\ + 19 \\ \hline \end{array}$$ s

Find the sum that matches each number below. Write the letters next to those sums on the lines below to solve this riddle.

How can you go without sleep
for seven days and not get tired?

Get ____ ____ ____ ____
52 95 63 93

____ ____ ____ ____ ____
55 90 42 71 81

____ ____
62 51

____ ____ ____ ____ ____
50 76 33 80 72

Squirrel Olympics

Welcome to the Squirrel Olympics! Regroup and add to find out how many acorns each squirrel gathers on its race down the hill. Who will get the most nuts and win the gold?

Add. Each sum becomes the top number of the next problem.

Shaggytail

$$\begin{array}{r} 18 \\ +\ 9 \\ \hline \end{array}$$

$$\begin{array}{r} +18 \\ \hline \end{array}$$

$$\begin{array}{r} +\ 8 \\ \hline \end{array}$$

$$\begin{array}{r} +\ 9 \\ \hline \end{array}$$

$$\begin{array}{r} +19 \\ \hline \end{array}$$

Nutley

$$\begin{array}{r} 19 \\ +\ 7 \\ \hline \end{array}$$

$$\begin{array}{r} +\ 9 \\ \hline \end{array}$$

$$\begin{array}{r} +18 \\ \hline \end{array}$$

$$\begin{array}{r} +19 \\ \hline \end{array}$$

$$\begin{array}{r} +18 \\ \hline \end{array}$$

Limbhopper

Rodentia

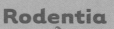

```
    9
  + 9
  ___
```

```
    7
  + 9
  ___
```

```
  + 18
  ____
```

```
  + 19
  ____
```

```
  + 9
  ___
```

```
  + 19
  ____
```

```
  + 17
  ____
```

```
  + 18
  ____
```

```
  + 9
  ___
```

```
  + 8
  ___
```

The winner is _____!

Seal Sums

Circle the two numbers that add up to the number on each seal.

25

9   14   15   16

35

15   16   17   18

57

26   28   29   31

21

7   8   10   13

24

4   7   14   17

46

19   25   27   31

Regroup Again . . . and Again!

You need to regroup when adding some three-digit numbers. Here's how it works.

1. Add the **ones** column first, and regroup.

$$\begin{array}{r} \overset{1}{3}87 \\ +\ 275 \\ \hline 2 \end{array}$$

2. Add the tens column. Include the number you regrouped from the ones column. If the sum of the tens column is greater than 9, regroup the number, and write it in the hundreds place, like this.

$$\begin{array}{r} \overset{1}{3}\overset{1}{8}7 \\ +\ 275 \\ \hline 62 \end{array}$$

3. Next add the hundreds column. Be sure to include the number you regrouped from the tens column.

$$\begin{array}{r} \overset{1}{3}\overset{1}{8}7 \\ +\ 275 \\ \hline 662 \end{array}$$

If the sum of the hundreds column is greater than 9, regroup the number, and write it like this. Then add the thousands column. In this case, there is only one number in the thousands column. Hint: Don't forget the comma.

$$\begin{array}{r} \overset{1}{6}\overset{1}{8}4 \\ +\ 553 \\ \hline 1,237 \end{array}$$

Add these numbers.

555	758	348	673	589
+ 266	+ 199	+ 262	+ 842	+ 277
t	r	e	o	t

364	672	733	464	578
+ 385	+ 429	+ 188	+ 468	+ 96
t	t	e	i	p

642	258	307	787	563
+ 159	+ 287	+ 905	+ 175	+ 472
i	h	d	o	t

509	185	834	726	388
+ 275	+ 676	+ 315	+ 159	+ 476
a	N	n	b	o

535	949	505	745	288
+ 199	+ 333	+ 550	+ 156	+ 359
r	e	e	e	r

Find the sum that matches each number below. Write the letters next to those sums on the lines below to solve this riddle.

Is it better to do your math homework on a full stomach or on an empty stomach?

___ ___ ___ ___ ___ ___ ___.
861   901   932   866   545   610   734

It is ___ ___ ___ ___ ___ ___
885   921   821   1,035   1,282   957

___ ___ ___ ___ ___ ___ ___ ___
749   1,515   1,212   864   801   1,101   962   1,149

___ ___ ___ ___ ___!
674   784   674   1,055   647

Mixed Addition

Losing a tooth is special. To find out what happens to kids' teeth in other parts of the world, add these numbers. Then circle the description above the sum that is different in each set of equations.

The Yupik people, Alaska

Hidden in meat and fed to a dog	Hidden in fruit and fed to your father	Hidden in candy and fed to your brother
32 + 40	26 + 36	43 + 19

Costa Rica

Made into a gold earring	Sewn into your pillowcase	Hung over your bed
86 + 89	110 + 40	87 + 63

Greece

Thrown into a fire	Thrown onto your roof	Thrown at your best friend
320 + 160	456 + 274	253 + 227

South Africa

Left in a basket, where a mouse will fall and then become your pet

225
+ 125

Left next to your toothbrush, so a mouse will leave you a new one

154
+ 196

Left in a slipper so a mouse will take it and leave you a gift

368
+ 82

Malaysia

Buried in the ground

586
+ 414

Dropped into a bird's nest

222
+ 578

Tied to a balloon and released into the sky

440
+ 360

What do you do with your teeth when they fall out?

_____

_____

Regroup and Subtract

Sometimes when you subtract two-digit numbers, you need to **regroup** to find the difference easily.

1. Look at the ones column. Can you subtract, or do you need to regroup first?

```
   4 5
 - 2 8
 _____
```

2. To regroup, look at the top number. Subtract 1 from the tens place, as shown. Add that 10 to the ones column.

```
   ³4̸¹5
 - 2 8
 _____
```

3. Subtract the ones column.

```
   ³4̸¹5
 - 2 8
 _____
```

4. Then subtract the tens column. Write your answer in the blue box.

```
   ³4̸¹5
 - 2 8
 _____
       7
```

Subtract these numbers.

```
    45          30          65          74
  - 17        - 12        - 49        - 28
  _____      _____      _____      _____
     r           a           u           a
```

$$
\begin{array}{r} 57 \\ -\ 19 \\ \hline \end{array}
$$
n

$$
\begin{array}{r} 88 \\ -\ 49 \\ \hline \end{array}
$$
d

$$
\begin{array}{r} 92 \\ -\ 56 \\ \hline \end{array}
$$
r

$$
\begin{array}{r} 32 \\ -\ 17 \\ \hline \end{array}
$$
o

$$
\begin{array}{r} 74 \\ -\ 67 \\ \hline \end{array}
$$
i

$$
\begin{array}{r} 61 \\ -\ 48 \\ \hline \end{array}
$$
A

$$
\begin{array}{r} 70 \\ -\ 56 \\ \hline \end{array}
$$
e

$$
\begin{array}{r} 76 \\ -\ 8 \\ \hline \end{array}
$$
d

$$
\begin{array}{r} 84 \\ -\ 57 \\ \hline \end{array}
$$
t

$$
\begin{array}{r} 42 \\ -\ 34 \\ \hline \end{array}
$$
c

$$
\begin{array}{r} 50 \\ -\ 38 \\ \hline \end{array}
$$
l

$$
\begin{array}{r} 94 \\ -\ 88 \\ \hline \end{array}
$$
p

Find the difference that matches each number below.
Write the letters next to those differences on the
lines below to solve this riddle.

What do you call a snowman in the summer?

___ ___ ___ ___ ___ ___ ___
13   8   18   36   28   15   27

___ ___ ___
7   38   46

___ ___ ___ ___ ___ ___!
6   16   39   68   12   14

More Regrouping

Subtract these numbers
using regrouping.

```
   27
 -  8
 _____
        o
```

```
   32
 - 26
 _____
        f
```

```
   45
 - 17
 _____
        m
```

```
   82
 - 25
 _____
        o
```

```
   90
 - 81
 _____
        m
```

```
   93
 - 46
 _____
        s
```

```
   78
 - 19
 _____
        d
```

```
   66
 - 48
 _____
        i
```

55
− 17
———
m

42
− 27
———
f

58
− 49
———
y

51
− 24
———
n

75
− 46
———
u

53
− 19
———
r

63
− 39
———
c

34
− 17
———
p

Find the difference that matches each number below.
Write the letters next to those differences to solve this riddle.

What happens when a vampire catches a cold?

His ____ ____ ____ ____ ____ gives him
   38   29   9   28   9

____ ____ ____ ____ ____ ____
24   57   15   6   18   27

____ ____ ____ ____ ____!
59   34   19   17   47

Solving Riddles

Use regrouping to subtract these numbers. Look for matching differences in the box to find the answer to each riddle.

What do you get if your sheep studies karate?

$$\begin{array}{r} 53 \\ -\ 46 \\ \hline \end{array}$$

What disappears when you turn on the light?

$$\begin{array}{r} 63 \\ -\ 26 \\ \hline \end{array}$$

What gets wetter the more it dries?

$$\begin{array}{r} 95 \\ -\ 28 \\ \hline \end{array}$$

What belongs to you but is used more by others?

$$\begin{array}{r} 52 \\ -\ 24 \\ \hline \end{array}$$

What can go around the world without leaving the corner?

$$\begin{array}{r} 67 \\ -\ 18 \\ \hline \end{array}$$

What kind of umbrella does your teacher carry on a rainy day?

$$\begin{array}{r} 78 \\ -\ 19 \\ \hline \end{array}$$

What goes up but doesn't come down?

$$\begin{array}{r} 32 \\ -\ 16 \\ \hline \end{array}$$

Which side of the chicken has the most feathers?

$$\begin{array}{r} 87 \\ -\ 68 \\ \hline \end{array}$$

Forward I am heavy; backward I am not. What am I?

$$\begin{array}{r} 46 \\ -\ 17 \\ \hline \end{array}$$

What two things run around together all day and spend all night with their tongues hanging out?

$$\begin{array}{r} 53 \\ -\ 14 \\ \hline \end{array}$$

Your name

$$\begin{array}{r} 91 \\ -\ 63 \\ \hline \end{array}$$

A stamp

$$\begin{array}{r} 73 \\ -\ 24 \\ \hline \end{array}$$

A towel

$$\begin{array}{r} 84 \\ -\ 17 \\ \hline \end{array}$$

Your age

$$\begin{array}{r} 90 \\ -\ 74 \\ \hline \end{array}$$

A ton

$$\begin{array}{r} 64 \\ -\ 35 \\ \hline \end{array}$$

A lamb chop

$$\begin{array}{r} 84 \\ -\ 77 \\ \hline \end{array}$$

A wet one

$$\begin{array}{r} 80 \\ -\ 21 \\ \hline \end{array}$$

The dark

$$\begin{array}{r} 75 \\ -\ 38 \\ \hline \end{array}$$

Your sneakers

$$\begin{array}{r} 64 \\ -\ 25 \\ \hline \end{array}$$

The outside

$$\begin{array}{r} 35 \\ -\ 16 \\ \hline \end{array}$$

Witch Number

School's out at Shiverview Elementary.
Help the Broom Buses deliver the right number
of kids to each stop. Solve the equations using regrouping.

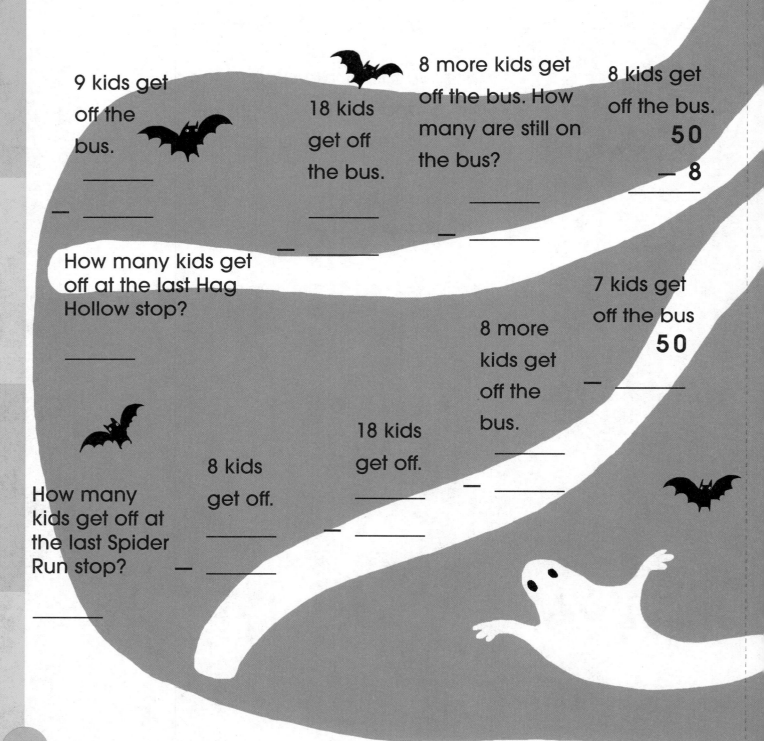

9 kids get off the bus.

_____

− _____

18 kids get off the bus.

_____

− _____

8 more kids get off the bus. How many are still on the bus?

_____

− _____

8 kids get off the bus.

50

− 8

_____

How many kids get off at the last Hag Hollow stop?

_____

7 kids get off the bus

50

− _____

_____

8 more kids get off the bus.

_____

− _____

How many kids get off at the last Spider Run stop?

8 kids get off.

_____

− _____

_____

18 kids get off.

_____

− _____

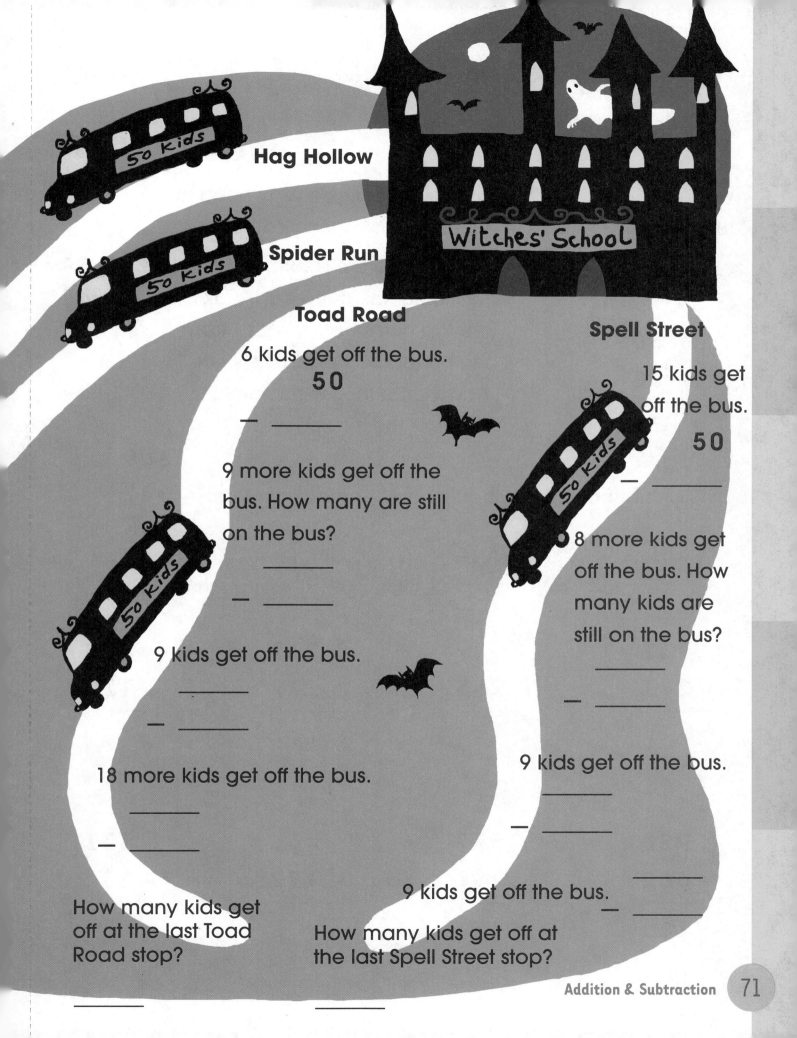

Hag Hollow

Spider Run

Witches' School

Toad Road

6 kids get off the bus.

50

− _____

9 more kids get off the
bus. How many are still
on the bus?

_____

− _____

9 kids get off the bus.

_____

− _____

18 more kids get off the bus.

_____

− _____

How many kids get
off at the last Toad
Road stop?

_____

Spell Street

15 kids get
off the bus.

50

− _____

8 more kids get
off the bus. How
many kids are
still on the bus?

_____

− _____

9 kids get off the bus.

_____

− _____

9 kids get off the bus.

How many kids get off at
the last Spell Street stop?

_____

Regroup Again . . . and Again!

When you subtract three-digit numbers, you may need to regroup to find the difference. Here is how you do it.

1. Subtract the ones column.

$$
\begin{array}{r}
569 \\
- 387 \\
\hline
2
\end{array}
$$

2. Regroup before subtracting the tens column. To regroup, look at the top number. Subtract 1 from the hundreds place, as shown. Add that to the tens column. Subtract the tens column.

$$
\begin{array}{r}
\overset{4}{\cancel{5}}{}^{1}69 \\
- 387 \\
\hline
82
\end{array}
$$

3. Subtract the numbers in the hundreds column.

$$
\begin{array}{r}
\overset{4}{\cancel{5}}{}^{1}69 \\
- 387 \\
\hline
182
\end{array}
$$

Subtract these three-digit numbers using regrouping.

$$
\begin{array}{r}
732 \\
- 271 \\
\hline
\,\text{h}
\end{array}
\qquad
\begin{array}{r}
649 \\
- 265 \\
\hline
\,\text{l}
\end{array}
\qquad
\begin{array}{r}
217 \\
- 72 \\
\hline
\,\text{e}
\end{array}
\qquad
\begin{array}{r}
322 \\
- 170 \\
\hline
\,\text{p}
\end{array}
$$

$$
\begin{array}{r}
928 \\
- 662 \\
\hline
\,\text{n}
\end{array}
\qquad
\begin{array}{r}
577 \\
- 281 \\
\hline
\,\text{r}
\end{array}
\qquad
\begin{array}{r}
465 \\
- 192 \\
\hline
\,\text{y}
\end{array}
\qquad
\begin{array}{r}
777 \\
- 282 \\
\hline
\,\text{e}
\end{array}
$$

$$419 - 255 = \text{(c)}$$
$$832 - 790 = \text{(l)}$$
$$611 - 490 = \text{(t)}$$
$$572 - 192 = \text{(a)}$$
$$377 - 159 = \text{(n)}$$

$$932 - 808 = \text{(t)}$$
$$750 - 675 = \text{(e)}$$
$$413 - 86 = \text{(e)}$$
$$100 - 47 = \text{(w)}$$
$$722 - 148 = \text{(a)}$$

$$817 - 628 = \text{(y)}$$
$$640 - 294 = \text{(s)}$$
$$888 - 99 = \text{(o)}$$
$$562 - 275 = \text{(o)}$$
$$342 - 184 = \text{(c)}$$

Find the difference above that matches each number below. Write the letters next to those differences on the lines below to solve this riddle.

There were ten cats in a boat. One jumped out.
How many cats were left in the boat?

___ ___ ___ ___ .   ___ ___ ___ ___
218 789 266 495   124 461 327 273

___ ___ ___ ___   ___ ___ ___
53   145 296 75   380 384 42

___ ___ ___ ___ ___ ___ ___ ___ !
158 287 152 189 164 574 121 346

Mixed Subtraction

Circle the difference that is not the same as the others in the set to answer the question.

How many hours a day does a koala sleep?

$$\begin{array}{r} 700 \\ -\ 685 \\ \hline \end{array}$$

$$\begin{array}{r} 47 \\ -\ 32 \\ \hline \end{array}$$

$$\begin{array}{r} 83 \\ -\ 61 \\ \hline \end{array}$$

How many pounds of chocolate on average does a person in the United States eat each year?

$$\begin{array}{r} 52 \\ -\ 45 \\ \hline \end{array}$$

$$\begin{array}{r} 980 \\ -\ 929 \\ \hline \end{array}$$

$$\begin{array}{r} 351 \\ -\ 344 \\ \hline \end{array}$$

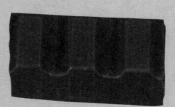

How many feet high was the tallest saguaro cactus ever measured?

$$710 - 652$$

$$108 - 66$$

$$990 - 948$$

How many motorcycles are in the world's largest motorcycle museum? (The Barber Vintage Motorsport in Alabama)

$$500 - 172$$

$$442 - 65$$

$$764 - 436$$

What's the greatest number of legs ever counted on a millipede?

$$653 - 529$$

$$811 - 687$$

$$907 - 197$$

A Handy Math Trick

You can check your answer to a subtraction equation by adding. Add the **difference** to the number you **subtracted**. You should get the number you **subtracted from**.

$$32 - 18 = 14$$

$$14 + 18 = 32$$

Solve these subtraction equations.
Write the addition equations next to them to check your answers.

$$42 - 18 = \underline{\qquad} \qquad + \underline{\qquad}$$

$$97 - 56 = \underline{\qquad} \qquad + \underline{\qquad}$$

$$456 - 362 = \underline{\qquad} \qquad + \underline{\qquad}$$

$$85 - 27 = \underline{\qquad} \qquad + \underline{\qquad}$$

322
− 92   +
_____   _____

788
− 555   +
_____   _____

253
− 172   +
_____   _____

50
− 17   +
_____   _____

180
− 26   +
_____   _____

56
− 48   +
_____   _____

630
− 416   +
_____   _____

Mixed Addition and Subtraction

Dig in to the equations below the pirate.

$$\begin{array}{r} 91 \\ -\ 65 \\ \hline \end{array}$$

$$\begin{array}{r} 14 \\ +\ 66 \\ \hline \end{array}$$

$$\begin{array}{r} 80 \\ -\ 56 \\ \hline \end{array}$$

$$\begin{array}{r} 63 \\ -\ 19 \\ \hline \end{array}$$

$$\begin{array}{r} 44 \\ +\ 92 \\ \hline \end{array}$$

$$\begin{array}{r} 146 \\ -\ 52 \\ \hline \end{array}$$

$$\begin{array}{r} 39 \\ +\ 62 \\ \hline \end{array}$$

$$\begin{array}{r} 101 \\ -\ 87 \\ \hline \end{array}$$

```
   24          52         136          47
 + 28        - 19        - 89        - 29
 ____        ____        _____       _____


   64         127          88          82
 - 25        - 63        + 39        + 56
 ____        ____        _____       _____


  106          18          49          98
 - 24        + 88        + 11        +  7
 ____        ____        _____       _____


   61         138          63          77
 + 27        - 77        + 14        - 25
 ____        ____        _____       _____
```

Spilled Milk

Oh, no! Look what the cat did! Fill in the numbers or symbols that were splashed by the spilled milk.

Remember:

If you know	then you know	
8 + 2 ――― 10	10 − 2 ――― 8	10 − 8 ――― 2

$$\begin{array}{r} 7 \\ -\ \_ \\ \hline 2 \end{array}$$

$$\begin{array}{r} \_\ \_ \\ +\ 8 \\ \hline 12 \end{array}$$

$$\begin{array}{r} 13 \\ +\ \_\ \_ \\ \hline 27 \end{array}$$

$$\begin{array}{r} 58 \\ 29 \\ \hline 28 \end{array}$$

$$\begin{array}{r} \_\ \_ \\ -\ 33 \\ \hline 54 \end{array}$$

$$\begin{array}{r} 40 \\ +\ \_\ \_ \\ \hline 83 \end{array}$$

$$\begin{array}{r} +14 \\ \hline 36 \end{array}$$

$$\begin{array}{r} 77 \\ + \\ \hline 94 \end{array}$$

$$\begin{array}{r} 34 \\ + 67 \\ \hline 67 \end{array}$$

$$\begin{array}{r} 82 \\ 8 \\ \hline 90 \end{array}$$

$$\begin{array}{r} -14 \\ \hline 50 \end{array}$$

$$\begin{array}{r} +137 \\ \hline 400 \end{array}$$

Word Problems

Read the problems. Then answer the questions by filling in the correct bubble.

1. Clara and Franki Ann have the same birth date. They decided to have a birthday party at an ice-skating rink. Clara invited 8 friends. Franki Ann invited 7 friends. How many friends did they invite altogether?

What does this word problem ask you to find?

a. ◯ Who invited more friends?

b. ◯ How many more friends did Clara invite than Franki Ann?

c. ◯ What is the total number of friends Clara and Franki Ann invited?

d. ◯ How many kids will be at the party, including Clara and Franki Ann?

Which equation could you use to find the answer?

a. ◯ addition: 8 + 7 = _____

b. ◯ subtraction 8 − 7 = _____

2. Including Clara and Franki Ann, 14 kids came to the birthday party. There were 3 kids who had their own ice skates. How many pairs of ice skates had to be rented?

What does this word problem ask you to find?

a. ◯ How many kids came to the party?

b. ◯ How many kids had their own skates?

c. ◯ How many kids needed rental skates?

d. ◯ How much will it cost to rent the skates?

Which equation could you use to find the answer?

a. ◯ addition: 14 + 3 = _____

b. ◯ subtraction: 14 − 3 = _____

3. The 14 kids skated for an hour. Then Clara's dad invited them to decorate cupcakes. There were 8 kids who went with Clara's dad. The rest wanted to skate some more. How many kids kept skating? Write an equation to solve this problem. Circle your answer.

4. Clara's dad baked a cupcake for each of the 14 kids. He also baked 10 extras. How many cupcakes were there altogether? Write an equation to solve this problem. Circle your answer.

5. Of the 14 kids, 10 drank milk with their cupcakes. The rest wanted water. How many kids drank water? Write an equation to solve this problem. Circle your answer.

Tricky Kids

Beware! One of these kids is trying to trick you! Read their word problems carefully. Write an equation for each one, and (circle) your answer. Then draw a mustache on the kid who tried to trick you!

My goal is to try every flavor at the ice cream shop. They sell 31 flavors. I've tried 17 already. How many flavors are left for me to try?

_____

My mom found a great sale on cat food and bought 40 cans. My dad saw the same sale and bought 50 cans. How many cans of cat food did they buy altogether?

_____

I have 35 math equations to solve. Yesterday I solved 20 math equations. How many more do I need to solve?

_____

For my birthday, my brother bought me 12 balloons. Unfortunately, it was a windy day, and all but 4 blew away. How many did I have left?

_____

My old Pogo-stick record was 349 jumps. Today I made 52 more jumps than that. What's my new Pogo-stick record?

_____

Yesterday I began reading my favorite book. I read 35 pages. Today I read 29 more pages and finished the book. How many pages long is my favorite book?

_____

It All Adds Up!

There once was a prince who loved candy bars. Every night after supper, his father, the king, called for the royal candy maker to wheel in his cart.

"Eat only 5 candy bars, dear," the queen would say.

"No fair!" the prince said.

He frowned while he was chewing.

The candy maker did not like people to frown while they ate his candy bars! He came up with a plan.

"My dear king and queen," he said. "I will make the prince a special candy bar for his birthday tomorrow. It will be the best, thickest candy bar he has ever had."

"Just one candy bar?" the prince demanded.

"Well," said the candy maker. "Since it is your eighth birthday, I will bring you tasty candy bars for 8 days."

The prince clapped his hands.

"And beginning the second day," explained the candy maker, "I will give you twice as many candy bars as you got the day before."

The prince started jumping up and down.

"All I ask," said the candy maker, "is that you promise to eat every candy bar I bring."

The prince wildly shook his head yes. He thought to himself:

Day 1 1 candy bar

Day 2 1 + 1 = _____ candy bars

Day 3 _____ + _____ = _____ candy bars

Day 4 _____ + _____ = _____ candy bars

The prince could see that by day 4 he would have more than 5 candy bars. Things would only get better from there! A big smile spread across his sticky face.

The candy maker showed up every day, just as he had promised. The prince gobbled up his candy bars on the first, second, and third days. On the fourth day, he was thrilled with his extra candy bars.

But on day 5, the prince began to feel funny. On day 6, he felt sick. On day 7, he turned green. On day 8, he burst out in tears. "May I please have just *one* candy bar?"

The candy maker quickly agreed. He handed the prince one candy bar and kept the others in his cart.

"Thank you," said the prince. He smiled through every bite.

Why did the prince get so sick of candy bars?
Hint: How many candy bars did he get on days 5, 6, and 7?
Write the equations for all the days here to find out.

Day 1 1

Day 2 1 + 1 = _____

Day 3 _____ + _____ = _____

Day 4 _____ + _____ = _____

Day 5 _____ + _____ = _____

Day 6 _____ + _____ = _____

Day 7 _____ + _____ = _____

Day 8 _____ + _____ = _____

Addition Game

Play this game with a partner.

1. Choose a number from 1 to 15.

2. Point to each lily pad on which your number appears.

3. Ask your partner to guess your number.

Take turns. How fast can you go?

1
3
5
7
9
11
13
15

2
3
6
7
10
11
14
15

8
9
10
11
12
13
14
15

4
5
6
7
12
13
14
15

Secret Message: This game is a trick! To guess your partner's number, add the top numbers on the pads your partner points to.

Addition & Subtraction Answer Key

Note: Answers read across, per page.

36–37 5 + 4 = 9, 3 + 3 = 6, 10 + 2 = 12, 10 + 10 = 20; 4; 5 + 5, 10 + 0, 8 + 2, 4 + 6, 3 + 7, 11 – 1, 14 – 4, 9 + 1, 0 + 10, 7 + 3, 1 + 9, 2 + 8, 6 + 4; 13; +, 0, 1, –, 14, –, 10, 8, 4, 7; 2; 3, 6, 6, 7, 3, 7, 10, 8, 4, 7; 3; belt

38–39 9, 16, 14, 12, 11; 3, 4, 1, 7; answers will vary but must add up to 7, 12, 16.

40–41 5, 4, 1, 2, 6, 3; **see below.**

42–43 4, 17, 7, 16, 8, 14, 10, 13, 9, 12, 14, 14, 16, 15, 6, 15, 14, 13, 14, 17, 5, 18, 18, 19, 15, 18, 17, 11, 12, 16; pumpkin for a coach!

44–45 36, 34, 58, 24, 99, 77, 59, 97, 93, 88, 69, 44, 95, 79, 68, 57, 42, 89, 87, 84, 96, 78, 66, 73, 54, 39

46–47 21, 63, 45, 43, 50, 27, 15, 12, 73, 11, 75, 71, 23, 14, 40, 25, 65, 44

48–49 374, 874, 668, 989, 598, 588, 668, 571, 777, 768, 995, 891, 916, 498, 976, 678, 773, 779, 659, 765, 945, 884, 808, 977; Boy, you sure have a lot of problems, don't you!

50–51 222, 523, 314, 10, 223, 202, 152, 110, 232, 121, 102, 132, 415, 562, 32,1, 214, 402, 443, 122, 433, 277, 301, 24; Because it makes the oil boil and the urn burn

52–53 42, 95, 50, 81, 76, 73, 53, 64, 96, 74, 61, 82, 75, 80, 91, 30, 51, 70, 54, 71; really big pair of hands

54–55 63, 33, 62, 93, 90, 71, 51, 76, 95, 81, 72, 52, 80, 50, 42, 55; your sleep at night

56–57 Shaggytail: 27, 45, 53, 62, 81; Nutley: 26, 35, 53, 72, 90; Limbhopper: 18, 36, 45, 62, 71; Rodentia: 16, 35, 54, 72, 80; Nutley

58–59 Circle 9, 16; 17, 18; 28, 29; 8, 13; 7, 17; 19, 27

60–61 821, 957, 610, 1,515, 866, 749, 1,101, 921, 932, 674, 801, 545, 1,212, 962, 1,035, 784, 861, 1,149, 885, 864, 734, 1,282, 1,055, 901, 647; Neither; better to do it on paper

62–63 The different number in each grouping should be circled. 72, 62, 62; 175, 150, 150; 480, 730, 480; 350, 350, 450; 1,000, 800, 800; answers will vary.

64–65 17; 28, 18, 16, 46, 38, 39, 36, 15, 7, 13, 14, 68, 27, 8, 12, 6; A carrot in a puddle

66–67 19, 6, 28, 57, 9, 47, 59, 18, 38, 15, 9, 27, 29, 34, 24, 17; mummy, coffin drops

68–69 7, 37, 67, 28, 49, 59, 16, 19, 29, 39; 28, 49, 67, 16, 29, 7, 59, 37, 39, 19

70–71 **Hag Hollow:** 42, 42 – 8 = 34, 34 – 18 = 16, 16 – 9 = 7, 7; **Spider Run:** 50 – 7 = 43, 43 – 8 = 35, 35 – 18 = 17, 17 – 8 = 9, 9; **Toad Road:** 50 – 6 = 44, 44 – 9 = 35, 35 – 9 = 26, 26 – 18 = 8, 8; **Spell Street:** 50 – 15 = 35, 35 – 8 = 27, 27 – 9 = 18, 18 – 9 = 9, 9

72–73 461, 384, 145, 152, 266, 296, 273, 495, 164, 42, 121, 380, 218, 124, 75, 327, 53, 574, 189, 346, 789, 287, 158; None. They were all copycats

74–75 The different number in each grouping should be circled. 15, 15, 22; 7, 51, 7; 58, 42, 42; 328, 377, 328; 124, 124, 710

76–77 24, 24 + 18 = 42; 41, 41 + 56 = 97; 94, 94 + 362 = 456; 58, 58 + 27 = 85; 230, 230 + 92 = 322; 233, 233 + 555 = 788; 81, 81 + 172 = 253; 33, 33 + 17 = 50; 154, 154 + 26 = 180; 8, 8 + 48 = 56; 214, 214 + 416 = 630

78–79 26, 80, 24, 44, 136, 94, 101, 14, 52, 33, 47, 18, 39, 64, 127, 138, 82, 106, 60, 105, 88, 61, 77, 52

80–81 5, 4, 14, –, 87, 43, 22, 17, 33, +, 64, 263

82–83 1. c, a (15); 2. c, b (11), 3. 14 – 8 = 6, 4. 14 + 10 = 24, 5. 14 – 10 = 4

84–85 31 – 17 = 14, 40 + 50 = 90, 35 – 20 = 15, 4 (this was the trick problem!), 349 + 52 = 401, 35 + 29 = 64

86–87 Day 2: 2, Day 3: 2 + 2 = 4, **Day 4:** 4 + 4 = 8, **Day 5:** 8 + 8 = 16, **Day 6:** 16 + 16 = 32, **Day 7:** 32 + 32 = 64

40–41

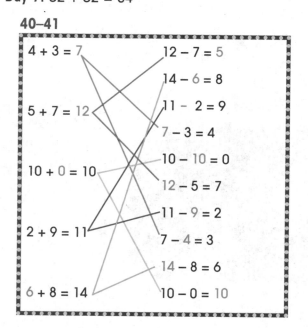

Repeat + Repeat + Repeat = Multiply!

Multiplication is a quick way to add the same number over and over.

The answer to a multiplication equation is called the **product**.

How many legs do 4 kids have?

2 + 2 + 2 + 2 = _____

2 + 2 + 2 + 2 is the same as 4 groups of 2.

It can be written as a multiplication equation:

4×2 = _____.

How many legs do 2 dogs have?

4 + 4 = _____

4 + 4 is the same as 2 groups of _____.

It can be written as a multiplication equation:

$2 \times$ _____ = _____.

Solve these addition equations.
Then write them as multiplication equations.

How many rabbit ears?

 = _____

_____ × _____ = _____

How many flowers?

 = _____

_____ × _____ = _____

How many starfish arms in all?

 = _____

_____ × _____ = _____

How many skateboard wheels are there?

 = _____

_____ × _____ = _____

How many spots?

 = _____

_____ × _____ = _____

My, Oh, My, Let's Multiply!

Draw pictures for each set of objects. Then write the numbers that show the problem in groups as a repeat addition equation. Finally, write the numbers as a multiplication equation. The first problem has been done for you.

Draw 4 groups of 3 matching hats.

$3 + 3 + 3 + 3 = 12$

$4 \times 3 = 12$

Draw 2 groups of 7 balls.
Write the addition and multiplication equations.

Draw 6 groups of 5 triangles.
Write the addition and multiplication equations.

Draw 4 groups of 6 stars.
Write the addition and multiplication equations.

Draw 3 groups of 3 squares.
Write the addition and multiplication equations.

Draw 10 groups of 2 mittens.
Write the addition and multiplication equations.

Hurray for Arrays!

Here is another way to show 3 × 6. This arrangement is called an array.

columns

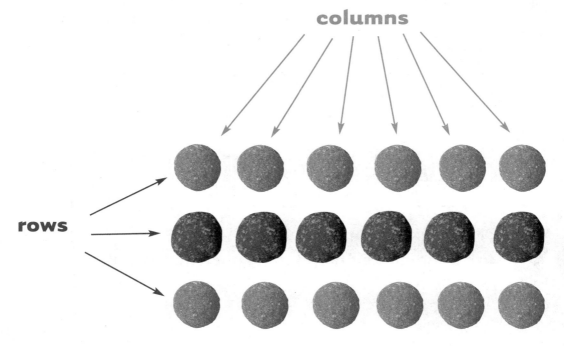

rows

There are _____ side-to-side rows.

There are _____ up-and-down columns.

Write multiplication equations for these arrays. (Hint: How many rows total? How many columns total?) Then solve the equations.

_____ × _____ = _____

_____ × _____ = _____

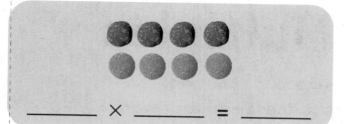

_____ × _____ = _____

_____ × _____ = _____

_____ × _____ = _____

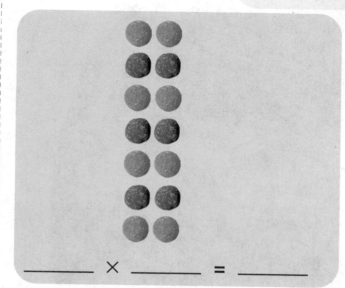

_____ × _____ = _____

_____ × _____ = _____

_____ × _____ = _____

_____ × _____ = _____

Draw an array of stars for this multiplication equation.

$2 \times 5 =$ _____

Counting by Multiples

You can do multiplication using skip counting.
Skip count to find the answers to these equations.
Then write a multiplication equation for each one.

You baked 5 pies. You used 10 apples to make each pie.
How many apples did you use altogether?

10, 20, _____, _____, _____

5 × 10 = _____

Your family rents 3 rowboats. Each boat seats 4 people. How many people altogether can ride in the boats?

_____, _____, _____

4 × 3 = _____

You trick-or-treated at 15 houses last Halloween. You got 2 pieces of candy at each house. How many pieces of candy did you get altogether?

————, ————, ————, ————, ————, ————, ————,

————, ————, ————, ————, ————, ————, ————, ————

———— × ———— = ————

On each of the 7 days last week, you sent 5 E-mails. How many E-mails did you send altogether?

————, ————, ————, ————, ————, ————, ————

———— × ———— = ————

You bought 3 boxes of toy cars. Each box had 3 cars in it. How many toy cars did you buy?

————, ————, ————

———— × ———— = ————

You have 4 friends coming over. Each friend is bringing 1 game to play. How many games will you have to choose from?

————, ————, ————, ————

———— × ———— = ————

Here's a Tricky One!
You check out 3 library books. Each one has 0 mouse characters in it. How many mice will you read about?

0, ————, ————

3 × 0 = ————

Two, Too Much!

Color in the multiples of 2. Hint: Use skip counting
to find the multiples of 2: 2, 4, 6, and so on.

1	2	3	4	5	6	7	8	9	10
11	12	13	14	15	16	17	18	19	20
21	22	23	24	25	26	27	28	29	30
31	32	33	34	35	36	37	38	39	40
41	42	43	44	45	46	47	48	49	50
51	52	53	54	55	56	57	58	59	60
61	62	63	64	65	66	67	68	69	70
71	72	73	74	75	76	77	78	79	80
81	82	83	84	85	86	87	88	89	90
91	92	93	94	95	96	97	98	99	100

Fill in the missing numbers to complete these multiplication facts.

$2 \times 1 =$ _____

$2 \times 2 =$ _____

$2 \times 3 =$ _____

_____ $\times 4 = 8$

$2 \times$ _____ $= 10$

$2 \times 6 =$ _____

_____ $\times 7 = 14$

$2 \times 8 =$ _____

$2 \times 9 =$ _____

$2 \times$ _____ $= 20$

$2 \times 11 =$ _____

$2 \times 12 =$ _____

What patterns do you see in these multiplication facts?

_____

_____

Cover the facing page. Time yourself to see how quickly you can solve these multiplication equations.

$10 \times 2 =$ _____ $2 \times 6 \ =$ _____

$3 \times 2 =$ _____ $2 \times 2 \ =$ _____

$2 \times 4 =$ _____ $8 \times 2 \ =$ _____

$2 \times 7 =$ _____ $2 \times 11 =$ _____

$2 \times 1 =$ _____ $5 \times 2 \ =$ _____

$12 \times 2 =$ _____ $2 \times 9 \ =$ _____

Study the multiplication facts again. Cover your other work on this page. Time yourself to see how quickly you can solve these multiplication equations.

$2 \times 5 \ =$ _____ $2 \times 3 \ =$ _____

$4 \times 2 \ =$ _____ $9 \times 2 \ =$ _____

$2 \times 2 \ =$ _____ $2 \times 8 \ =$ _____

$2 \times 12 =$ _____ $1 \times 2 \ =$ _____

$6 \times 2 \ =$ _____ $2 \times 10 =$ _____

$11 \times 2 \ =$ _____ $7 \times 2 \ =$ _____

Give Me Five!

Color in the multiples of 5. Hint: Skip counting by 5s will help you.

1	2	3	4	5	6	7	8	9	10
11	12	13	14	15	16	17	18	19	20
21	22	23	24	25	26	27	28	29	30
31	32	33	34	35	36	37	38	39	40
41	42	43	44	45	46	47	48	49	50
51	52	53	54	55	56	57	58	59	60
61	62	63	64	65	66	67	68	69	70
71	72	73	74	75	76	77	78	79	80
81	82	83	84	85	86	87	88	89	90
91	92	93	94	95	96	97	98	99	100

Fill in the missing numbers to complete these multiplication facts.

$5 \times 1 =$ _____

$5 \times 2 =$ _____

$5 \times 3 =$ _____

_____ $\times 4 = 20$

$5 \times$ _____ $= 25$

$5 \times 6 =$ _____

$5 \times 7 =$ _____

$5 \times$ _____ $= 40$

$5 \times 9 =$ _____

$5 \times 10 =$ _____

$5 \times$ _____ $= 55$

$5 \times 12 =$ _____

What patterns do you see in these multiplication facts?

_____

_____

Cover the facing page. Time yourself to see how quickly you can solve these multiplication equations.

10 × 5 = _____   5 × 6 = _____

3 × 5 = _____   2 × 5 = _____

5 × 4 = _____   8 × 5 = _____

5 × 7 = _____   5 × 11 = _____

5 × 1 = _____   5 × 5 = _____

12 × 5 = _____   5 × 9 = _____

Study the multiplication facts again. Cover your other work on this page. Time yourself to see how quickly you can solve these multiplication equations.

5 × 5 = _____   5 × 3 = _____

4 × 5 = _____   9 × 5 = _____

5 × 2 = _____   5 × 8 = _____

5 × 12 = _____   1 × 5 = _____

6 × 5 = _____   5 × 10 = _____

11 × 5 = _____   7 × 5 = _____

Ten, Again and Again!

Color in the multiples of 10. Hint: Skip counting by 10s will help you.

1	2	3	4	5	6	7	8	9	10
11	12	13	14	15	16	17	18	19	20
21	22	23	24	25	26	27	28	29	30
31	32	33	34	35	36	37	38	39	40
41	42	43	44	45	46	47	48	49	50
51	52	53	54	55	56	57	58	59	60
61	62	63	64	65	66	67	68	69	70
71	72	73	74	75	76	77	78	79	80
81	82	83	84	85	86	87	88	89	90
91	92	93	94	95	96	97	98	99	100

Fill in the missing numbers to complete these multiplication facts.

$10 \times 1 =$ _____

$10 \times 2 =$ _____

$10 \times$ _____ $= 30$

$10 \times 4 =$ _____

$10 \times 5 =$ _____

_____ $\times 6 = 60$

$10 \times 7 =$ _____

$10 \times$ _____ $= 80$

$10 \times 9 =$ _____

$10 \times 10 =$ _____

$10 \times$ _____ $= 110$

$10 \times 12 =$ _____

What patterns do you see in these multiplication facts?

_____

_____

Cover the facing page. Time yourself to see how quickly you can solve these multiplication equations.

10 × 10 = _____   10 × 6 = _____

3 × 10 = _____   2 × 10 = _____

10 × 4 = _____   8 × 10 = _____

10 × 7 = _____   10 × 11 = _____

10 × 1 = _____   5 × 10 = _____

12 × 10 = _____   10 × 9 = _____

Study the multiplication facts again. Cover your other work on this page. Time yourself to see how quickly you can solve these multiplication equations.

10 × 5 = _____   10 × 3 = _____

4 × 10 = _____   9 × 10 = _____

10 × 2 = _____   10 × 8 = _____

10 × 12 = _____   1 × 10 = _____

6 × 10 = _____   10 × 10 = _____

11 × 10 = _____   7 × 10 = _____

Mixed Multiplication

January
_____
National Static Electricity Day
3 × 3

January
_____
National Handwriting Day
3 × 4

January
_____
National Dress-Up-Your-Pet Day
7 × 2

January
_____
National Nothing Day
2 × 8

March
_____
Everything You Do Is Right Day
8 × 2

March
_____
Rotten Sneaker Day
4 × 5

March
_____
Make Up Your Own Holiday Day
2 × 13

May
_____
Kite Day
2 × 2

May
_____
Limerick Day
2 × 6

May
_____
Straw Hat Day
5 × 3

May
_____
National Tap-Dance Day
5 × 5

October
_____
National Grouch Day
3 × 5

October
_____
Reptile Awareness Day
5 × 4

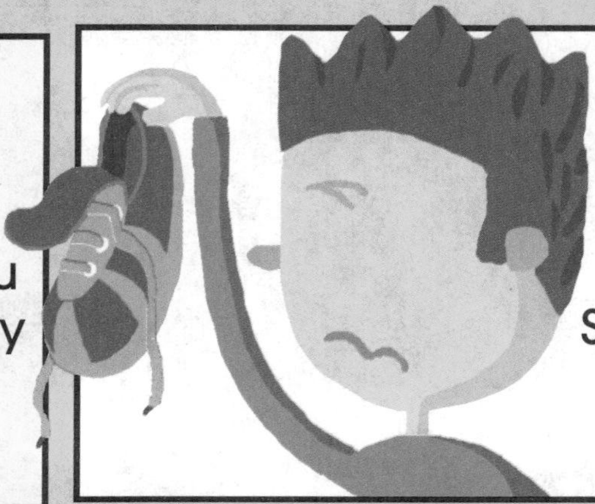

Want a reason to celebrate? Multiply these numbers to find the dates of some wacky holidays.

January
_____
Squirrel Appreciation Day
3 × 7

February
_____
International Pancake Day

March
_____
Middle-Name Pride Day
2 × 4

April
_____
National Sense-of-Smell Day
4 × 2

April
_____
National Siblings Day
2 × 5

April
_____
No Socks Day
2 × 14

April
_____
National Toasted-Marshmallow Day
5 × 6

June
_____
National Yo-Yo Day
3 × 2

July
_____
National Cousins Day
2 × 12

September
_____
Swap Ideas Day
5 × 2

September
_____
Video Games Day
6 × 2

November
_____
National Teddy Bear Day
2 × 7

December
_____
Games Day
2 × 10

Repeat-Repeat-Repeat = Division!

You can use subtraction to solve division equations.

You have a basket of 15 apples. Each kid can eat 3 apples. How many kids will the basket feed?

Imagine that kids line up and take apples out of the basket 3 at a time.

15 apples − 3 apples = 12 apples left

12 apples − 3 apples = _____ apples left

_____ apples − 3 apples = _____ apples left

_____ apples − 3 apples = _____ apples left

_____ apples − 3 apples = _____ apples left

How many kids did the basket of apples feed? _____

Repeat subtraction is the same as **division**. Here's how you would write the problem as a division equation:

$$15 \div 3 = \underline{\hspace{2cm}}$$

You have a box of 15 crackers. The crackers must be shared equally among 5 kids. How many crackers will each kid get? This time, imagine that you pass out a cracker to each kid on each round.

15   crackers –   5   crackers = _____ crackers left

_____ crackers – _____ crackers = _____ crackers left

_____ crackers – _____ crackers = _____ crackers left

How many crackers did each kid get? _____

Express the problem as a division equation: 15 ÷ 5 = _____

You have a jar of 100 marbles. If each kid gets 20 marbles, how many kids can share the marbles in the jar?
Use this set of subtraction equations to solve the problem.

100   marbles –   20   marbles = _____ marbles left

_____ marbles – _____ marbles = 60 marbles left

60   marbles – _____ marbles = _____ marbles left

_____ marbles –   20   marbles = 20 marbles left

_____ marbles – _____ marbles = _____ marbles left

How many kids got marbles? _____

Express the problem as a division equation:

_____ ÷ _____ = _____

Equal Sharing

Here's another way to do division. These lines show how you would divide this box of chocolates equally among 3 people.

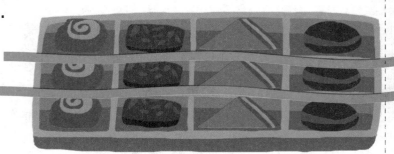

Each person gets _____.

12 ÷ 3 = _____

Draw lines to show how you would divide this equally among 4 people. (Hint: Your dividing lines can go up and down, too.)

Each person gets _____.

12 ÷ 4 = _____

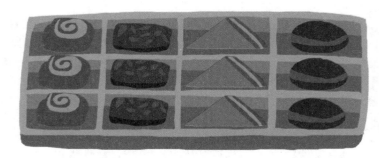

Draw a line to show how you would divide this equally between 2 people.

Each person gets _____.

12 ÷ 2 = _____

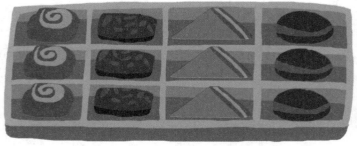

Draw lines to show how you would divide this equally among 6 people.

Each person gets _____.

12 ÷ 6 = _____

Draw pictures to help solve these two equations.

You have 10 dog biscuits. How can you share them between 2 dogs?

Each dog gets _____ biscuits.

10 ÷ 2 = _____

You have 10 dog biscuits. How can you share them among 5 dogs?

Each dog gets _____ biscuits.

10 ÷ 5 = _____

Can you divide these beach balls equally between 2 people? If you can, complete the division equation. If you can't, cross out the equation.

1 ÷ 2 = _____

2 ÷ 2 = _____

3 ÷ 2 = _____

4 ÷ 2 = _____

5 ÷ 2 = _____

6 ÷ 2 = _____

7 ÷ 2 = _____

8 ÷ 2 = _____

9 ÷ 2 = _____

10 ÷ 2 = _____

What do you notice about the numbers you can divide by 2?

_____

A number that can be used to divide another number evenly is called its **factor**.

What kind of numbers have 2 as a factor?

_____

Remainders

Just because you can't divide a number evenly doesn't mean you can't divide it at all. You just have to write how many are left over after you find the equal share.

How can you share 7 carrots between 2 rabbits?

The rabbits get _____ carrots apiece.

How many carrots are left over? _____

This number is called the **remainder**.

Express this as a division equation:

$$\underset{\text{carrots}}{7} \div \underset{\text{rabbits}}{2} = \underset{\substack{\text{carrots} \\ \text{per rabbit}}}{\rule{2cm}{0.4pt}} \text{r.} \underset{\text{remainder}}{\rule{2cm}{0.4pt}}$$

Divide 11 bananas among 3 gorillas.

The gorillas get _____ bananas apiece.

There is a remainder of _____ bananas.

$$\underset{\text{bananas}}{\rule{2cm}{0.4pt}} \div \underset{\text{gorillas}}{\rule{2cm}{0.4pt}} = \underset{\substack{\text{bananas} \\ \text{per gorilla}}}{\rule{2cm}{0.4pt}} \text{r.} \underset{\text{remainder}}{\rule{2cm}{0.4pt}}$$

Divide 19 crackers between 2 parrots.

The parrots get _____ crackers apiece.

There is a remainder of _____ cracker.

_____ ÷ _____ = _____ r. _____

Divide 8 slices of pizza among 3 boys.

The boys get _____ slices apiece.

There is a remainder of _____ slices.

_____ ÷ _____ = _____ r. _____

Divide 17 acorns among 5 squirrels.

The squirrels get _____ acorns apiece.

There is a remainder of _____ acorns.

_____ ÷ _____ = _____ r. _____

Fact Families

You may have guessed by now that multiplication and division are opposites, just like addition and subtraction.

If you know that
3 × 2 = 6,
then you know that
6 ÷ 3 = 2
and
6 ÷ 2 = 3.

If 5 × 8 = 40,

then _____ ÷ 8 = 5

and _____ ÷ 5 = 8.

If 70 ÷ 10 = 7,

then 70 ÷ 7 = _____

and 7 × 10 = _____.

If 1 × 9 = 9,

then 9 ÷ 9 = _____

and _____ ÷ 1 = 9.

If 12 ÷ 4 = 3,

then 4 × 3 = _____

and 12 ÷ 3 = _____.

Complete these multiplication facts.
Write two division facts you know about these numbers.

$2 \times 4 = $ _____
a

$5 \times 3 = $ _____
k

$3 \times 2 = $ _____
p

$4 \times 1 = $ _____
a

$1 \times 5 = $ _____
M

$4 \times 5 = $ _____
u

$5 \times 2 = $ _____
p

$2 \times 7 = $ _____
c

$3 \times 4 = $ _____
l

$2 \times 8 = $ _____
s

Find the answer that matches each number below. On the lines,
write the letters that appear below the answers.

How do you divide 11 apples among 12 kids?

_____ a _____ e
  5   15

_____ _____ _____ _____ e _____ _____ _____ _____ e
  4   10   6   12   16   8   20   14

Camping Problems

Read the word problems. Answer the questions by filling in the correct bubble or following the directions.

1. Elise has 4 flashlights. Each flashlight needs 2 C batteries. If Elise needs all of the flashlights for her camping trip, how many batteries does she need to buy?

What does this word problem ask you to find?

a. ○ How many flashlights does Elise have?

b. ○ How many C batteries are needed to power 1 flashlight?

c. ○ How many C batteries are needed to power 4 flashlights?

d. ○ How many people are going on the camping trip?

Which equation can you use to find the answer?

a. ○ multiplication: $4 \times 2 =$ _____

b. ○ division: $4 \div 2 =$ _____

2. Elise bought a pack of 12 AA batteries. It takes 4 AA batteries to power a portable radio. How many portable radios can Elise's batteries power?

What does this word problem ask you to find?

a. ○ How many AA batteries are in each package?

b. ○ How many AA batteries are in each portable radio?

c. ○ How many portable radios does Elise need for her camping trip?

d. ○ How many portable radios can 12 AA batteries power?

Which equation can you use to find the answer?

a. ○ multiplication: $12 \times 4 =$ _____

b. ○ division: $12 \div 4 =$ _____

3. There are 4 family members, including Elise, on the camping trip. Each one wants 3 toasted marshmallows. How many marshmallows do they need altogether?

Write an equation to solve this problem. Circle your answer.

_____

4. Elise caught 8 fish. If she divides the fish among the 4 people on the trip (including her), how many fish will each person eat?

Write an equation to solve this problem. Circle your answer.

_____

5. All 4 people sleep in tents. Each tent sleeps 2 people. How many tents does Elise's family need?

Write an equation to solve this problem. Circle your answer.

_____

More Tricky Kids

Those tricky kids are back! Read their word problems carefully.
Write an equation for each one, and circle your answer.
Then draw a mustache on the kid who tried to trick you.

I have 12 dog rain booties. When I take my dogs out in the rain, they use all of them. Each dog wears 4 rain booties. How many dogs do I have?

_____

My 2 snakes just laid 5 eggs each. How many snakes do I have altogether?

_____

My cat won 10 blue ribbons at last year's pet shows. I hung them in 5 display cases. Each case has an equal number of ribbons. How many ribbons are in each display case?

_____

My 3 bunnies each eat 3 carrots a day. How many carrots altogether do I have to bring them each day?

_____

My 2 dogs chased a skunk, and now they stink! If I need 4 cans of tomato sauce to wash each dog, how many cans do I need altogether?

_____

My brother said that if I clean the cat's litter box all next week, he would clean it for twice as many days after that. Since there are 7 days in a week, for how many days will he have to clean it?

_____

Double Trouble

Use multiplication to save these characters from a haunted house!
Write the missing numbers on the lines.

"This house is haunted," I told my friend Jenny.

"My grandma said this house was once owned by Mrs. Meanie, the meanest teacher that ever lived," said Jenny. "Once when Grandma was little, she hid her favorite doll in her lunchbox. She brought it to school. When Mrs. Meanie found it, she took the doll away. I just want to find my grandma's doll."

"What if there are ghosts?" I asked.

"Follow me," Jenny said.

We walked into the living room. We could not believe our eyes. The room was filled with shelves of dusty toys.

"There's Grandma's doll!" Jenny cried. She lifted it from a shelf.

BAM! Suddenly, the front door slammed. CREAK, CREAK, CREAK! The floorboards in the hallway groaned.

"I'm scared!" I whispered.

"Look!" Jenny said. She pointed behind me. I turned and saw a wrinkled old woman with cobwebs in her hair. She had a ruler in her hand.

"Mrs. Meanie!" Jenny whispered.

"Put that doll back, young lady," Mrs. Meanie warned, "or your troubles will multiply!"

Jenny shook her head. "This doll belongs to my grandma."

"Very well," Mrs. Meanie said. She pointed her ruler at a shelf with 5 jack-in-the-boxes on it.

"Kazam, kazive, multiply by 5!"

Suddenly, _____ × _____ = _____ jack-in-the-boxes flew at us. They knocked dust onto our faces and hair.

Jenny hugged the doll tighter.

Mrs. Meanie pointed her ruler at a shelf with 5 yo-yos on it. "Fi, fo, fen, multiply by 10!" she said.

_____ × _____ = _____ yo-yos shot through the air. Jenny and I scrambled under a table.

There was a stuffed monkey on a shelf. Mrs. Meanie pointed her ruler at it next. "Fi, fo, fen, multiply by 10!" she cried.

_____ × _____ = _____ stuffed monkeys started jumping around us.

"Get Mrs. Meanie over here," I said. "I will do the rest."

Jenny nodded. "You can have the doll back!" she called out.

Mrs. Meanie frowned. "I can't hear you unless you raise your hand!" she snarled.

Jenny raised her hand. Mrs. Meanie took some shuffling steps over to our hiding place. She reached out her hand for the doll.

SNATCH! I grabbed the ruler and pointed it straight at her.

Mrs. Meanie laughed. "That ruler only multiplies," she said. "Why don't you try it? Say 'Boo, hoo, multiply by 2!' and you'll get double trouble."

"I already know that $2 × 1 =$ _____," I said, "but I also know about zero."

"You've been listening in class!" Mrs. Meanie wailed.

"Shazeero!" I shouted. "_____ × 1 = _____!"

Mrs. Meanie disappeared. So did all the toys, all except the doll Jenny was hugging. We ran out of the spooky house. We ran all the way to Jenny's grandma's house. She was happy to see her doll. She was even happier to see us!

Multiplication Game

You'll need a partner, a spinner (you can make one), the scorecards on this page, a paper clip, and a pencil.

1. The younger player goes first. Take turns spinning the paper clip. You will get 0, 1, 2, or 5.

2. Look at your scorecard. Choose the number that you want to multiply the number you spun by. (You are trying to get the highest score.) You can multiply each number on your scorecard only once. Before you decide, think: If you spin a 5, do you want to multiply it by a high number or a low number? What if you spin a 0?

3. Take turns until each scorecard is full. Then add up your points. (You can use a calculator.) The person with the highest score wins.

Make a spinner like this. Flick the paper clip. It will spin around the pencil point.

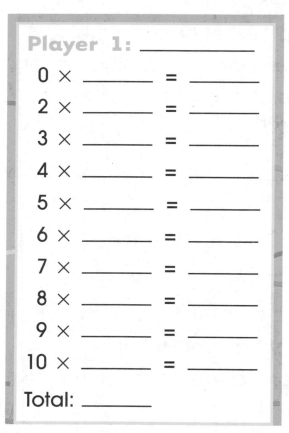

Player 1: _____

0 × _____ = _____
2 × _____ = _____
3 × _____ = _____
4 × _____ = _____
5 × _____ = _____
6 × _____ = _____
7 × _____ = _____
8 × _____ = _____
9 × _____ = _____
10 × _____ = _____

Total: _____

Player 2: _____

0 × _____ = _____
2 × _____ = _____
3 × _____ = _____
4 × _____ = _____
5 × _____ = _____
6 × _____ = _____
7 × _____ = _____
8 × _____ = _____
9 × _____ = _____
10 × _____ = _____

Total: _____

Multiplication & Division Answer Key

Note: Answers read across, per page, unless noted.

90–91 8, 8; 8, 4, 2 × 4 = 8; 10, 5 × 2 = 10; 9, 3 × 3 = 9; 20, 4 × 5 = 20; 12, 3 × 4 = 12; 18, 3 × 6 = 18

92–93 7 + 7 = 14, 2 × 7 = 14; 5 + 5 + 5 + 5 + 5 + 5 = 30, 6 × 5 = 30; 6 + 6 + 6 + 6 = 24, 4 × 6 = 24; 3 + 3 + 3 = 9, 3 × 3 = 9; 2 + 2 + 2 + 2 + 2 + 2 + 2 + 2 + 2 + 2 = 20, 10 × 2 = 20

94–95 3, 6; 4 × 3 = 12, 4 × 4 = 16, 2 × 4 = 8, 3 × 4 = 12, 1 × 7 = 7, 7 × 2 = 14, 5 × 3 = 15, 6 × 3 = 18, 5 × 7 = 35; draw 2 rows and 5 columns of stars.

96–97 30, 40, 50, 50; 4, 8, 12, 12; 2, 4, 6, 8, 10, 12, 14, 16, 18, 20, 22, 24, 26, 28, 30, 15 × 2 = 30; 5, 10, 15, 20, 25, 30, 35, 7 × 5 = 35; 3, 6, 9, 3 × 3 = 9; 1, 2, 3, 4, 4 × 1 = 4; 0, 0, 0

98–99 Color all numbers ending in 2, 4, 6, 8, 0; **answers by column:** 2, 4, 6, 2, 5, 12, 2, 16, 18, 10, 22, 24; all answers are even numbers, all end in 0, 2, 4, 6, or 8; 20, 6, 8, 14, 2, 24, 12, 4, 16, 22, 10, 18; 10, 8, 4, 24, 12, 22, 6, 18, 16, 2, 20, 14

100–101 Color all numbers ending in 5 or 0; **answers by column:** 5, 10, 15, 5, 5, 30, 35, 8, 45, 50, 11, 60; answers alternate between numbers ending in 5 (odd) and numbers ending in 0 (even); 50, 15, 20, 35, 5, 60, 30, 10, 40, 55, 25, 45; 25, 20, 10, 60, 30, 55, 15, 45, 40, 5, 50, 35

102–103 Color all numbers ending in 0; **answers by column:** 10, 20, 3, 40, 50, 10, 70, 8, 90, 100, 11, 120; all the answers are even numbers, a number multiplied times 10 equals the number with a 0 after it; 100, 30, 40, 70, 10, 120, 60, 20, 80, 110, 50, 90; 50, 40, 20, 120, 60, 110, 30, 90, 80, 10, 100, 70

104–105 **Answers by month:** 9, 12, 14, 16, 21, 12, 8, 16, 20, 26, 8, 10, 28, 30, 4, 12, 15, 25, 6, 24, 10, 12, 15, 20, 14, 20

106–107 9, 9, 6, 6, 3, 3, 0, 5, 5; 10, 10, 5, 5, 5, 5, 5, 0, 3, 3; 80, 80, 20, 20, 40, 40, 20, 20, 0, 5, 100 ÷ 20 = 5

108–109 4, 4; 3, 3; 6, 6; 2, 2; 5, 5; 2, 2; cross out problems with 1, 3, 5, 7, and 9 balls (other answers are 1, 2, 3, 4, 5); all numbers that can be divided by 2 are even; even numbers have 2 as their factor.

110–111 3, 1, 7 ÷ 2 = 3 r. 1; 3, 2, 11 ÷ 3 = 3 r. 2; 9, 1, 19 ÷ 2 = 9 r. 1; 2, 2, 8 ÷ 3 = 2 r. 2; 3, 2, 17 ÷ 5 = 3 r. 2

112–113 40, 40; 10, 70; 1, 9; 12, 4; 8, 8 ÷ 2 = 4, 8 ÷ 4 = 2; 15, 15 ÷ 5 = 3, 15 ÷ 3 = 5; 6, 6 ÷ 2 = 3, 6 ÷ 3 = 2; 4, 4 ÷ 1 = 4, 4 ÷ 4 = 1; 5, 5 ÷ 5 = 1, 5 ÷ 1 = 5; 20, 20 ÷ 4 = 5, 20 ÷ 5 = 4; 10, 10 ÷ 5 = 2, 10 ÷ 2 = 5; 14, 14 ÷ 2 = 7, 14 ÷ 7 = 2; 12, 12 ÷ 3 = 4, 12 ÷ 4 = 3; 16, 16 ÷ 2 = 8, 16 ÷ 8 = 2; M(a)k(e) appl(e)sauc(e)

114–115 1. c, a (4 × 2 = 8); 2. d, b (12 ÷ 4 = 3); 3. 4 × 3 = 12; 4. 8 ÷ 4 = 2 ; 5. 4 ÷ 2 = 2

116–117 12 ÷ 4 = 3; 2 (this is the trick question); 10 ÷ 5 = 2; 3 × 3 = 9; 2 × 4 = 8; 7 × 2 = 14

118–119 5 × 5 = 25, 5 × 10 = 50, 1 × 10 = 10, 2 × 1 = 2, 0 × 1 = 0

108–109

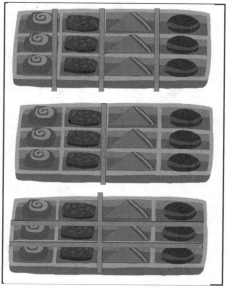

Half & Half

A **fraction** is a number that describes part of a whole.
If you divide something into 2 equal parts, each part is called **one-half**.

Here's how you write the fraction **one-half** using numbers: $\frac{1}{2}$

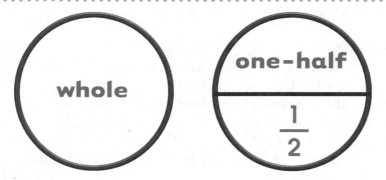

Draw lines to divide these shapes in half. Remember: Both parts must be equal. Hint: Your lines can run down, across, or side to side. Color each half a different color, and label it using numbers.

Now draw two real things that you might need to divide in half. Show the 2 equal parts.

The plural (more than one) of **half** is **halves**.

How many halves are in a whole? _____

A Third, a Third, and a Third

If you divide something into 3 equal parts, each part is called **one-third**. Here's how you write the fraction **one-third** using numbers: $\frac{1}{3}$

Draw lines to divide these shapes into equal thirds.

Color one of your shapes this way: $\frac{1}{3}$ **red**, $\frac{1}{3}$ yellow, and $\frac{1}{3}$ **blue**.

$\dfrac{1}{3}$ means **one-third**.

How would you write **two-thirds**? _____

How many thirds are in a whole? _____

Color another shape $\dfrac{2}{3}$ **red** and $\dfrac{1}{3}$ **blue**.

Color another shape $\dfrac{3}{3}$ yellow.

Going Forth with Fourths

If you divide something into 4 equal parts, each part is called **one-fourth**. Here's how you write the fraction one-fourth using numbers:

$$\frac{1}{4}$$

Put a ✓ next to the objects that are divided into fourths.

Color one of the shapes you checked this way:
$\frac{1}{4}$ red, $\frac{1}{4}$ yellow, $\frac{1}{4}$ blue, and $\frac{1}{4}$ green.

$\dfrac{1}{4}$ means one-fourth.

How would you write two-fourths? _____

How would you write three-fourths? _____

How many fourths are in a whole? _____

Color another shape $\dfrac{2}{4}$ **red** and $\dfrac{2}{4}$ **blue**.

Color another shape $\dfrac{3}{4}$ **yellow** and $\dfrac{1}{4}$ **green**.

Color another shape $\dfrac{4}{4}$ **purple**.

Halves, Thirds, Fourths

Help get these pizzas delivered to the correct customers.
Draw a line between each pizza and the person who ordered it.
His or her name will give you a hint

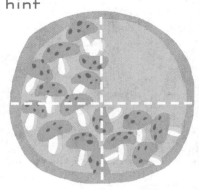

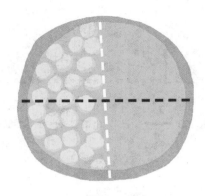

I. C. Stripes
My sweet pizza is divided into $\frac{2}{4}$ and $\frac{2}{4}$.

Ima Hongry
My pizza is $\frac{2}{2}$ plain but plenty for me.

Juan Topping
My whole pizza has $\frac{4}{4}$ of a creamy treat.

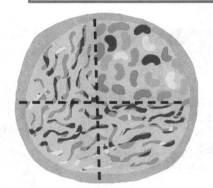

Arndt I. Healthy
My pizza is $\frac{1}{3}$ red, $\frac{1}{3}$ orange, and $\frac{1}{3}$ yellow.

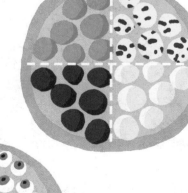

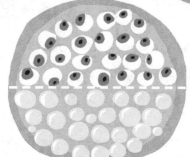

G. Rilla
My pizza topping is $\frac{2}{4}$ yellow fruit.

Frue Tinuts
$\frac{1}{2}$ of my pizza is as scary as the other $\frac{1}{2}$.

Ellie Phant
My nutty pizza is divided into $\frac{2}{3}$ and $\frac{1}{3}$.

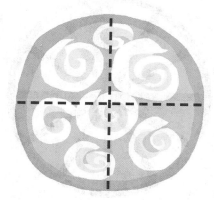

Svesh L. Order
Each $\frac{1}{4}$ of my topping is a different flavor . . . and it's melting!

I. E. Tefungi
$\frac{3}{4}$ of my pizza has the same plant on it.

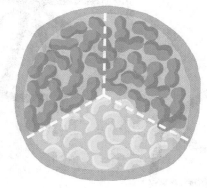

I. Ron Belly
My sweet pizza is divided into $\frac{3}{4}$ and $\frac{1}{4}$.

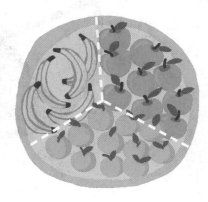

From Fifths to Twelfths

Write the correct fraction near the color section of each circle:

$$\frac{1}{5}, \frac{1}{6}, \frac{1}{7}, \frac{1}{8}, \frac{1}{9}, \frac{1}{10}, \frac{1}{11}, \frac{1}{12}$$

Now write each fraction name in words. For example:

$\frac{1}{5}$ **one-fifth**

$\frac{1}{6}$ _____

$\frac{1}{7}$ _____

$\frac{1}{8}$ _____

$\frac{1}{9}$ _____

$\frac{1}{10}$ _____

$\frac{1}{11}$ _____

$\frac{1}{12}$ _____

Fractions, Top to Bottom!

Numerator: How many of those equal parts you're talking about.

$$\frac{1}{8}$$

Denominator: How many equal parts in all.

Color these shapes to match the fractions.

Color $\frac{1}{7}$ **blue**.

Color $\frac{2}{5}$ **pink**.

Color $\frac{11}{12}$ **orange**.

Color $\frac{3}{5}$ **green**.

Color $\frac{4}{6}$ **yellow**.

Color $\frac{5}{11}$ **purple**.

Color $\frac{6}{8}$ **red**.

Color $\frac{9}{12}$ **yellow**.

Color $\frac{5}{10}$ **green**.

Color $\frac{7}{9}$ **blue**.

Color $\frac{3}{6}$ **purple**.

Color $\frac{3}{8}$ **brown**.

Color $\frac{3}{9}$ **red**.

Fractions & Groups

Part of a **group** can be shown as a fraction, too.

For example, if you had 5 friends who looked like this,

then $\dfrac{3}{5}$ of them are boys and $\dfrac{2}{5}$ of them are girls.

Finish these fractions.

What fraction of these firefighters have belts? $\dfrac{\square}{3}$

What fraction of these firefighters have fire hoses? $\dfrac{\square}{3}$

What fraction of these firefighters have hats? $\dfrac{\square}{3}$

What fraction of these pirates have hats? $\dfrac{\square}{4}$

What fraction of these pirates have peg legs? $\dfrac{\square}{4}$

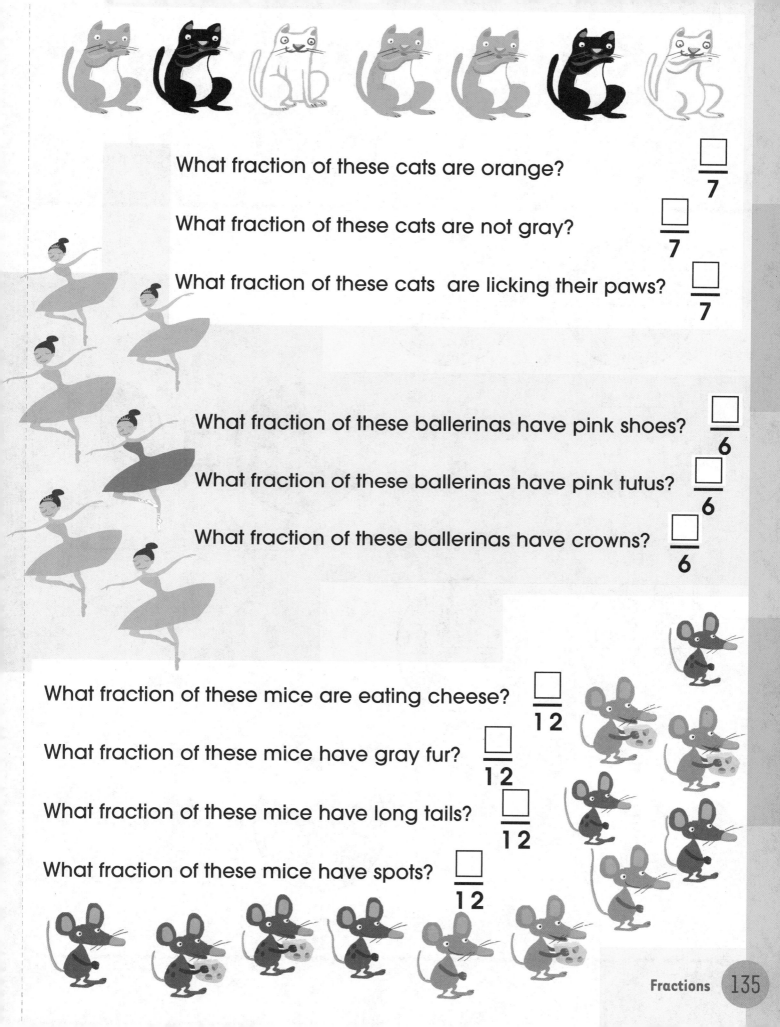

What fraction of these cats are orange? $\dfrac{\square}{7}$

What fraction of these cats are not gray? $\dfrac{\square}{7}$

What fraction of these cats are licking their paws? $\dfrac{\square}{7}$

What fraction of these ballerinas have pink shoes? $\dfrac{\square}{6}$

What fraction of these ballerinas have pink tutus? $\dfrac{\square}{6}$

What fraction of these ballerinas have crowns? $\dfrac{\square}{6}$

What fraction of these mice are eating cheese? $\dfrac{\square}{12}$

What fraction of these mice have gray fur? $\dfrac{\square}{12}$

What fraction of these mice have long tails? $\dfrac{\square}{12}$

What fraction of these mice have spots? $\dfrac{\square}{12}$

Comparing Fractions

The second grade had a pie-eating contest.
Compare what is left in each pair of pies. Write **>**, **<**, or **=** to show
the relationship. Then write the fractions underneath each pie.

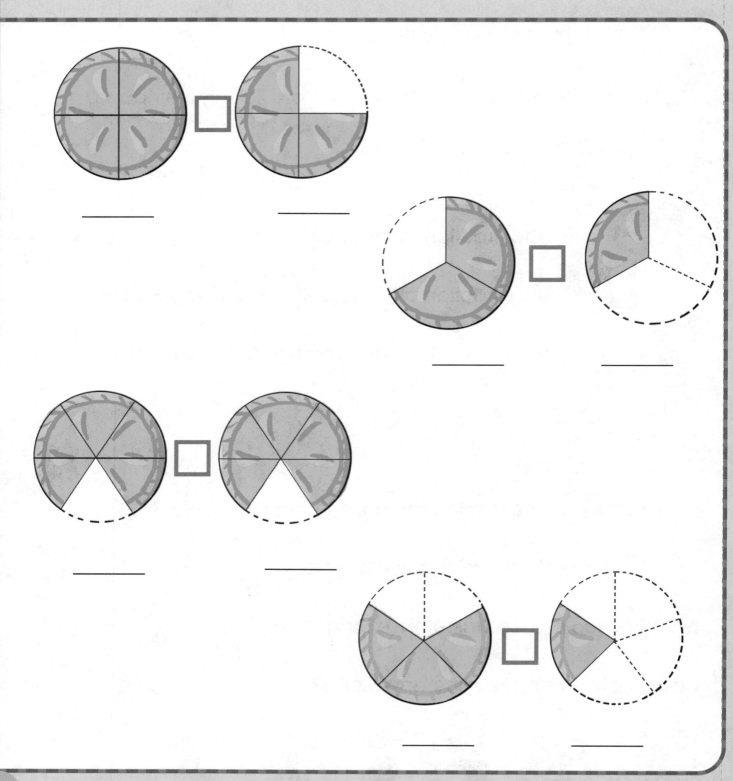

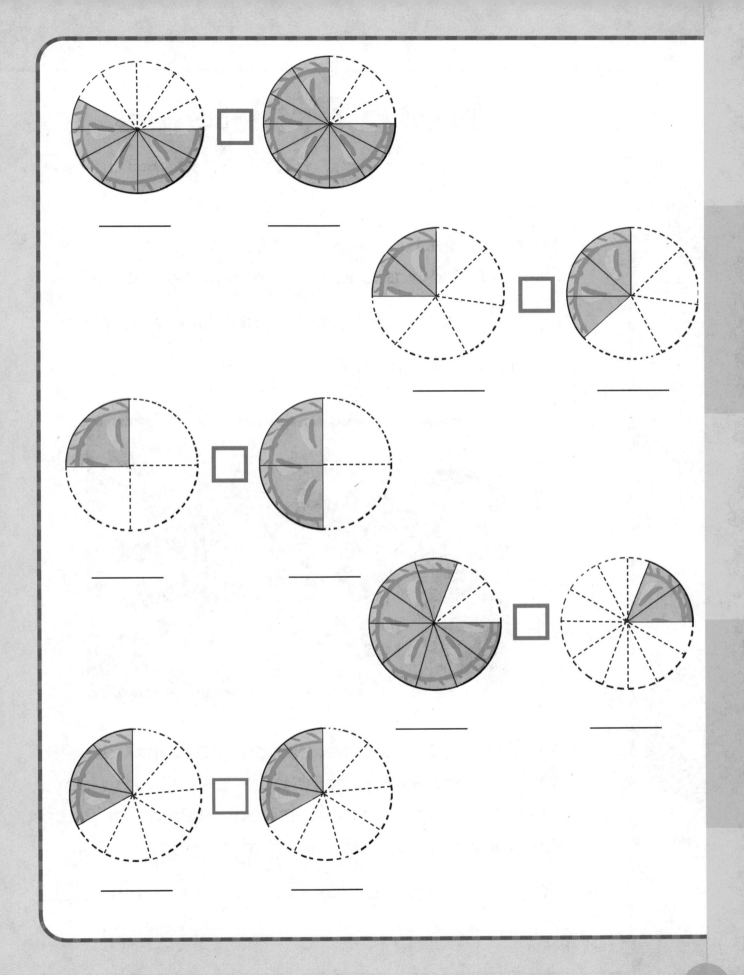

Word Problems

Solve these word problems. Write your answers as fractions.

1. Jake invited 5 friends to his birthday party. One friend was sick; the other 4 friends came.

What fraction of the kids Jake invited were able to come to his party? _____

2. Maria had 10 kids at her birthday party, including herself. In the middle of the party, 2 kids had to leave. Later, Maria's dad divided the cake into equal pieces, one for each kid who was still at the party.

What fraction of the cake did each guest eat? _____

3. Elise got 8 birthday presents: 2 books, 3 art kits, 1 soccer ball, 1 yo-yo, and 1 jump rope.

What fraction of her presents were art kits? _____

4. Tanya got 7 birthday presents: 3 books, 2 art kits, 1 computer game, and 1 T-shirt.

What fraction of her presents were **not** books? _____

5. Devin filled 9 party treat bags. He gave out 7 of the bags at his birthday party.

What fraction of the bags did he have left? _____

Fractions Game

You'll need a partner, paper, and crayons or markers.

1. Trace the pizza pie on this page on to a piece of paper. Do this for each game question below. Have your partner do the same thing.

2. Read the questions below out loud, one at a time. Draw and color in what you think is the answer on a pizza. Have your partner do the same thing. Check your answers by comparing drawings. If your drawing is correct, put a ✔ next to it. Whoever gets the most pizza pies wins!

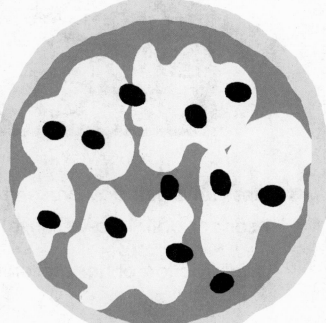

Game Questions

On these pizzas, which is bigger: $\dfrac{1}{2}$ or $\dfrac{1}{3}$?

On these pizzas, which is smaller: $\dfrac{2}{3}$ or $\dfrac{2}{4}$?

On these pizzas, which is bigger: $\dfrac{1}{6}$ or $\dfrac{1}{10}$?

On these pizzas, which is smaller: $\dfrac{2}{5}$ or $\dfrac{3}{4}$?

Play again with different fraction comparisons.

Fractions Answer Key

122–123 See below; drawings will vary (different options are shown with different colored lines); 2

124–125 See below; coloring may vary, but should reflect correct fraction; different third options

are shown with different colored lines; $\frac{2}{3}$, 3

126–127 See below; $\frac{2}{4}$, $\frac{3}{4}$; 4

128–129 See below.

130–131 $\frac{1}{9}$, $\frac{1}{12}$, $\frac{1}{10}$, $\frac{1}{11}$, $\frac{1}{5}$, $\frac{1}{7}$, $\frac{1}{6}$, $\frac{1}{8}$; one-sixth, one-seventh, one-eighth, one-ninth, one-tenth, one-eleventh, one-twelfth

132–133 See below; sections colored may vary, but should show correct fraction.

134–135 $\frac{2}{3}$, $\frac{1}{3}$, $\frac{3}{3}$; $\frac{3}{4}$, $\frac{2}{4}$; $\frac{3}{7}$, $\frac{5}{7}$, $\frac{6}{7}$; $\frac{5}{6}$, $\frac{5}{6}$, $\frac{4}{6}$; $\frac{5}{12}$, $\frac{5}{12}$, $\frac{7}{12}$, $\frac{5}{12}$

136–137 $\frac{4}{4} > \frac{3}{4}$; $\frac{2}{3} > \frac{1}{3}$; $\frac{5}{6} = \frac{5}{6}$; $\frac{3}{5} > \frac{1}{5}$; $\frac{7}{12} < \frac{9}{12}$; $\frac{2}{8} < \frac{3}{8}$; $\frac{1}{4} < \frac{2}{4}$; $\frac{8}{10} > \frac{2}{10}$; $\frac{3}{9} = \frac{3}{9}$

138–139 1. $\frac{4}{5}$, 2. $\frac{1}{8}$, 3. $\frac{3}{8}$, 4. $\frac{4}{7}$, 5. $\frac{2}{9}$

122–123

124–125

126–127

128–129

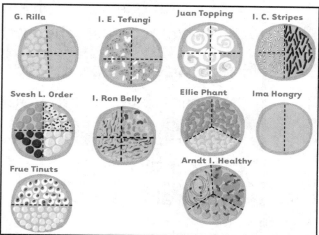

132–133

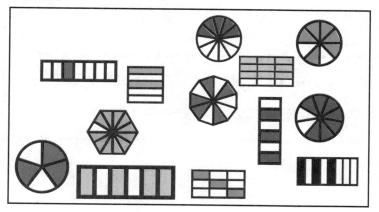

Sneaky Measures!

How many sneakers tall are you?
See how you measure up.

1. Lie flat on the floor with your feet against a wall or against a large piece of furniture, like a couch. Place a thick book directly above your head.

2. Get up carefully. The space between the book and the wall is about equal to your height.

3. Get a pair of sneakers, and measure the space like this: Start with one shoe against the wall. Put the other shoe directly in front of it on the floor. Pick up the first shoe and put it in front of the second shoe. Count as you go. When you get to the end, estimate a fraction if you need to. Write the number:

My height is _____ sneakers.

Choose 5 other items to measure your height with.
You can use one of these ideas, or choose your own.

the biggest book in your house   a toy car

the smallest book in your house   a roll of wrapping paper

a crayon   a spoon

a baseball bat   a doll

a football

Hint: If you're measuring with one tool, you can mark your place with your finger each time you move the tool.

Record your measurements in this list. The first line is the number. The second line is the name of the object you used to measure.

My height is _____ _____.

My height is _____ _____.

My height is _____ _____.

My height is _____ _____.

My height is _____ _____.

What else could these kids do? Write your answer on the lines.

My sneakers are bigger than yours. That means if we both use our own sneakers to measure something, we won't get the same answer. So, how can we compare our height?

We could measure with the same sneakers! Or we could

_____

_____

_____

_____

Slithery snake _____ inches long

Inch by Inch

Inches are a standard unit of measurement used in the United States. **Standard** means that the inches on the ruler on page 145 are the same size as the inches on every other ruler.

Cut out the ruler on page 145. Use it to measure the wizard school supplies on this page.

1. Make sure the inches side of your ruler is facing up.
2. Hold the ruler so that the edge is at one end of the object.
3. Read the number at the other end of the object. Write it on the line.

WART PASTE

Tube of wart paste

_____ inches long

Creepy bug _____ inches long

Magic wand

_____ inches long

Magic mirror

_____ inches wide

Candle stub _____ inches tall

TRICKS

Bag of tricks

_____ inches tall

1

2

3

4

5

6

7

8

— 1	
— 2	
— 3	
— 4	
— 5	
— 6	
— 7	
— 8	
— 9	
— 10	
— 11	
— 12	
— 13	
— 14	
— 15	
— 16	
— 17	
— 18	
— 19	
— 20	

Say It in Centimeters

Centimeters are another unit of measurement. They are part of the **metric system**. Scientists use the metric system. Most of the other countries in the world do, too. An **inch** equals about $2\frac{1}{2}$ centimeters.

Find the centimeter side of the ruler you cut out. Use it to measure the elf and fairy school supplies.

Fairy wand

_____ centimeters long

Fairy mushroom

_____ centimeters high and _____ centimeters wide

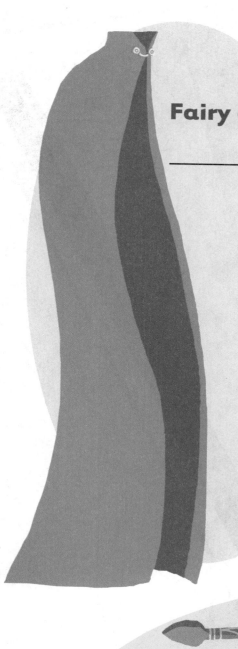

Fairy cape

_____ centimeters long

Elf shoe

_____ centimeters long

Elf staff _____ centimeters long

Magic elf rope _____ centimeters long

Estimate

You've used a ruler. Now measure with your eyes and brain. Estimate the length of each of these pictures. Fill in the bubble next to the correct answer. Hint: "in." stands for inches, and "cm" stands for centimeters.

○ 10 cm
○ 20 cm
○ 100 cm

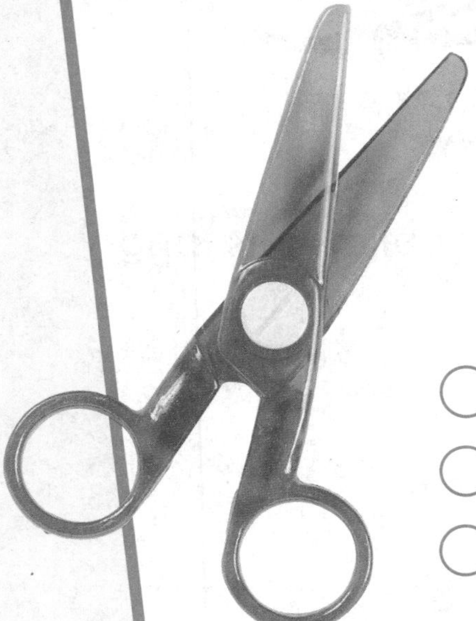

○ 3 in.
○ 5 in.
○ 10 in.

○ 6 cm
○ 14 cm
○ 10 cm

○ 100 cm
○ 5 cm
○ 10 cm

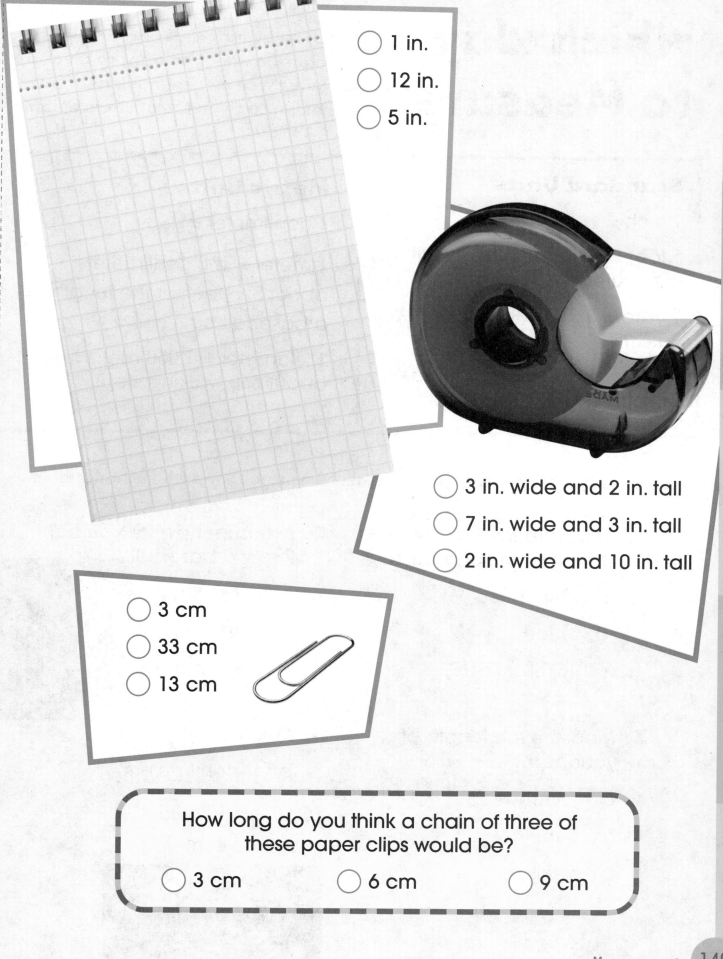

- ◯ 1 in.
- ◯ 12 in.
- ◯ 5 in.

- ◯ 3 in. wide and 2 in. tall
- ◯ 7 in. wide and 3 in. tall
- ◯ 2 in. wide and 10 in. tall

- ◯ 3 cm
- ◯ 33 cm
- ◯ 13 cm

How long do you think a chain of three of these paper clips would be?

◯ 3 cm   ◯ 6 cm   ◯ 9 cm

Which Way to Measure?

Which measuring unit or tool you use depends on what you want to measure. Look at these measuring units. They will help you fill in the answers below.

Standard Units

1 inch =

1 foot = 12 inches, the length of most rulers

1 yard = 3 feet, the length of a yardstick

1 mile = 5,280 feet, about 1,060 walking steps

Metric Units

1 centimeter =

1 meter = 100 centimeters, about $3\frac{1}{4}$ feet, or the length of a baseball bat

1 kilometer = 1,000 meters, about 660 walking steps

Choose the best unit for each measurement job, and fill in that bubble.

1. Measure the tallest block building you can build.

   d ◯ inches

   d ◯ feet

   r ◯ miles

2. Measure how far you can throw a baseball.

   a ◯ centimeters

   i ◯ meters

   a ◯ kilometers

3. Measure the length of your bed.

   l ◯ inches

   i ◯ feet

   e ◯ miles

4. Measure a bus ride.

   p ◯ centimeters

   n ◯ meters

   g ◯ kilometers

5. Measure a football field.

t ◯ inches

n ◯ yards

r ◯ miles

6. Measure a pet mouse.

t ◯ centimeters

n ◯ meters

s ◯ kilometers

7. Measure your thumb.

i ◯ inches

a ◯ feet

e ◯ miles

8. Measure a television screen.

n ◯ centimeters

t ◯ meters

s ◯ kilometers

9. Measure the width of North America.

l ◯ inches

i ◯ yards

t ◯ miles

10. Measure your foot.

n ◯ centimeters

m ◯ meters

f ◯ kilometers

11. Measure a train.

i ◯ inches

a ◯ feet

u ◯ miles

12. Measure a driveway.

i ◯ centimeters

s ◯ meters

a ◯ kilometers

Find the item number that matches each number below.
Write the letters next to the answers on the lines below to solve the riddle.

How many feet are there in a yard?

It depends on how many kids are

___ ___ ___ ___ ___ ___ ___ ___
12   9   11   10   1   7   5   4

___ ___ ___ ___!
3   8   2   6

Volume

Each of these containers holds a standard **volume**, or amount, of liquid. (Circle) the ones you've seen before. Look at the unit words beneath each one. Then use what you know to answer the questions. Fill in the bubble next to the correct answer.

1 cup

1 pint =
2 cups

1 quart =
4 cups

1 gallon =
16 cups

1 liter =
$1\frac{1}{10}$ quarts

---

1. Which of these is the largest unit of volume?

    o ◯ a pint   d ◯ a cup

    e ◯ a gallon   t ◯ a quart

2. Which of these is the smallest unit of volume?

    a ◯ a pint   o ◯ a cup

    e ◯ a gallon   i ◯ a quart

3. Which of these units is metric?

    s ◯ a pint   p ◯ a cup

    t ◯ a liter   f ◯ a quart

4. Which of these can you measure in cups?

    e ◯ time   t ◯ volume

    d ◯ distance   r ◯ weight

5. How many cups are in a gallon?

    t ◯ 2   g ◯ 8

    p ◯ 4   o ◯ 16

6. How many cups are in a pint?

    p ◯ 2   n ◯ 8

    m ◯ 4   d ◯ 16

7. How many cups are in a quart?

w ◯ 2   r ◯ 8

n ◯ 4   t ◯ 16

8. How many pints are in a quart?

! ◯ 2   + ◯ 8

? ◯ 4   = ◯ 16

9. How many quarts are in a gallon?

b ◯ 2   t ◯ 8

n ◯ 4   o ◯ 16

10. Which of these volumes of milk would you drink with a meal?

y ◯ 1 cup   e ◯ 1 gallon

r ◯ 1 quart   s ◯ 1 liter

11. These units can be used to measure other things you can pour, like sand and flour. Which of these units would you use when making a cake?

e ◯ cups   b ◯ gallons

12. About how many liters of soda would you buy for a party with 10 guests? (Hint: Most large soda bottles hold 2 liters.)

r ◯ 1   n ◯ 60

m ◯ 6   p ◯ 160

Find the item number that matches each number below. Write the letters or symbol next to the answers on the lines below to solve this riddle.

How many jelly beans can you put in an empty 1-liter soda bottle?

___ ___ ___
5   7   1

After that, it's

___ ___ ___
9   2   4

___ ___ ___ ___ ___ ___
11   12   6   3   10   8

Weigh In

Weight is measured in ounces, pounds, or tons.

Look at the examples. They will help you answer the questions below. Fill in the correct bubble for each question.

1 ounce
A letter with one first-class stamp weighs an ounce.

1 pound = 16 ounces
A guinea pig can weigh about a pound.

1 ton = 2,000 pounds
A baby elephant can weigh 1 ton.

1. Which of these is the largest unit of weight?

s ● a ton   t ○ a pound

n ○ an ounce

2. Which of these is the smallest unit of weight?

l ○ a ton   p ○ an ounce

n ● a pound

3. Which of these can you measure in pounds?

= ○ length   + ○ area

! ● weight   ? ○ volume

4. How many ounces are in 1 pound?

a ○ 2   o ● 16

e ○ 2,000

5. How many pounds are in a ton?

u ○ 2   e ○ 16

i ● 2,000

6. Which of these weighs 1 pound?

o ○ you   a ○ a horse

e ● a guinea pig

i ○ a fifth grader

7. Which of these could you eat at one sitting?

e ◯ 2 ounces of chocolate

a ◯ 2 pounds of chocolate

u ◯ 2 tons of chocolate

8. Which would you use to measure the weight of a goldfish?

n ◯ ounces   m ◯ pounds

r ◯ tons

9. Which would you use to measure the weight of a jet plane?

s ◯ ounces   t ◯ pounds

n ◯ tons

10. Which would you use to measure your own weight?

e ◯ ounces y ◯ pounds

t ◯ tons

11. Which is heavier?

t ◯ 20 ounces

p ◯ 1 pound

12. Which is heavier?

r ◯ 1,000 lbs

m ◯ 1 ton

Find the item number that matches each number below. Write the letters or symbol next to the answers on the lines below to solve the riddle.

How many pounds of dirt are there in a hole that's 4 feet deep, 4 feet long, and 3 feet wide?

___ ___ ___ ___ .
 9   4   8   6

A hole

___ ___
 5   1

___ ___ ___ ___ ___ ___
 7 12   2   11 10   3

Too Hot? Too Cold?

We measure temperature with a thermometer. Here's how to read a thermometer:

Fahrenheit

Celsius

1. The red line is a tube of liquid that rises when it is hot and falls when it is cold. Find the top of the red line. Find the closest black mark. What number is to the left of it? This is the Fahrenheit (F) temperature. What number is to the right? This is the metric Celsius (C) temperature.

2. If the mark doesn't have a number next to it, find the closest number below. Count up by two's as shown here. This thermometer reads 64°F.

Water freezes at 32°F and 0°C.

Color the line in for each thermometer to show the temperature in degrees.

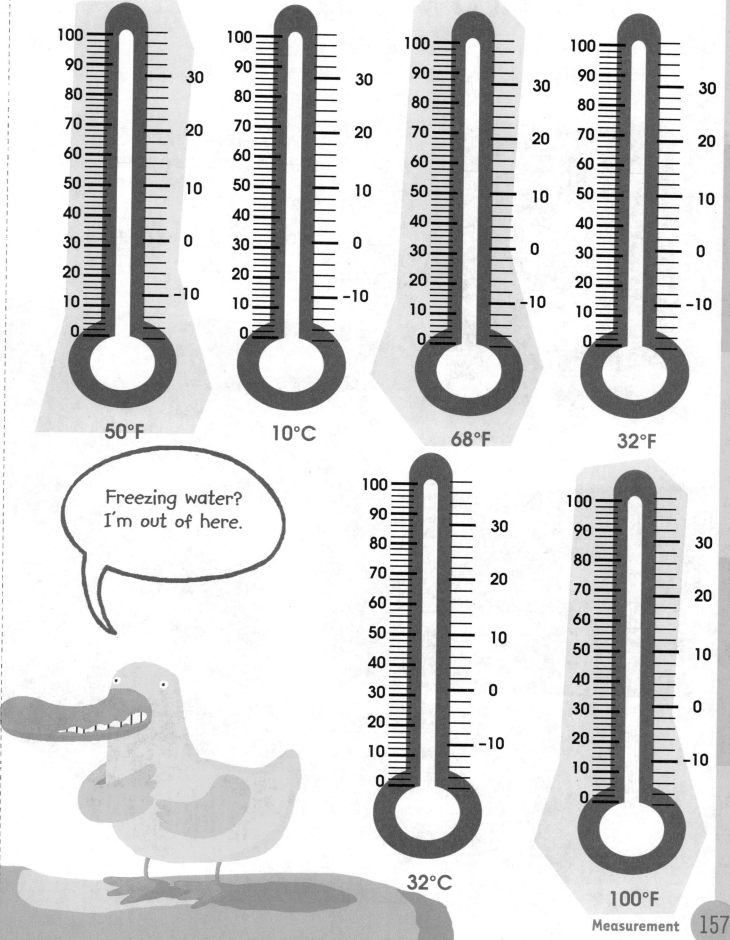

50°F

10°C

68°F

32°F

Freezing water? I'm out of here.

32°C

100°F

What to Wear?

Looking at a thermometer can help you decide how to dress for the day. Read the questions below. Fill in the bubble next to the correct answer.

The thermometer reads 80°F. Which would be most comfortable?

- ○ pants and long sleeves
- ○ a winter coat, hat, and mittens
- ● shorts and a T-shirt

The thermometer reads 30°F. Which would be most comfortable?

- ○ pants and long sleeves
- ● a winter coat
- ○ shorts and a T-shirt

The thermometer reads 50°F. Which would be most comfortable?

- ● a light jacket
- ○ a winter coat
- ○ a T-shirt

The thermometer reads 95°F. Which would be most comfortable?

- ○ a winter coat
- ○ pants and long sleeves
- ● a bathing suit

What's a good temperature for snow skiing?

- ◉ 25°F
- ○ 50°F
- ○ 75°F

What's a good temperature for water skiing?

- ○ 40°F
- ○ 60°F
- ◉ 80°F

What's a good temperature for throwing snowballs?

- ◉ 32°F
- ○ 93°F
- ○ 63°F

What's a good temperature for throwing a Frisbee at the beach?

- ○ 27°F
- ◉ 72°F
- ○ 17°F

What is the hottest temperature where you live? __90 F__ °

What is the coldest temperature where you live? __25 F__ °

Scavenger Hunt

Each player (or team of players) takes a copy of this list. The first to fill in the list wins the scavenger hunt!

You'll need a few players and the items listed below.

1. Something that's about 4 in. long: _____

2. Something that's about 4 cm long: _____

3. Something that's about 10 in. long: _____

4. Something that's about 15 cm long: _____

5. Something that's shorter than 1 centimeter: _____

6. Something that's longer than 1 foot: _____

7. Something that's colder than 32°F: _____

8. Something that can get hotter than 300°F: _____

9. Something that could be measured in cups: _____

10. Someone who weighs more than 100 lbs.: _____

Measurement Answer Key

142–143 Answers will vary. Kids may think of using a ruler or other standard measuring tool to compare their height.

144–145 **snake:** 7 inches; **warte paste:** 5 inches; **bug:** 4 inches; **wand:** 8 inches; **candle:** 3 inches; **mirror:** 2 inches; **bag:** 6 inches

146–147 **wand:** 6 centimeters; **mushroom:** 8 centimeters high and 5 centimeters wide; **cape:** 15 centimeters; **shoe:** 5 centimeters; **staff:** 12 centimeters; **rope:** 18 centimeters

148–149 **scissors:** 3 in.; **pencil:** 20 cm; **crayon:** 10 cm; **eraser:** 6 cm; **pad:** 5 in.; **tape dispenser:** 3 in. and 2 in.; **paper clip:** 3 cm; 9 cm

150–151 1. d, 2. i, 3. i, 4. g, 5. s, 6. t, 7. i, 8. n, 9. t, 10. n, 11. a, 12. s; are standing in it

152–153 1. e, 2. o, 3. t, 4. t, 5. o, 6. p, 7. n, 8. !, 9. n, 10. y, 11. e, 12. m; one; it's not empty!

154–155 1. s, 2. p, 3. !, 4. o, 5. i, 6. e, 7. e, 8. n, 9. N, 10. y, 11. t, 12. m; none; is empty!

156–157 **See below.**

158–159 shorts and a T-shirt, a winter coat, a light jacket, a bathing suit, 25°F, 80°F, 32°F, 72°F; answers will vary.

156–157

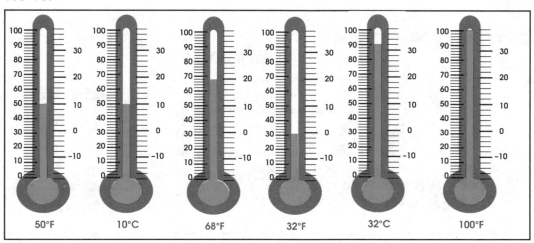

50°F   10°C   68°F   32°F   32°C   100°F

Wanted: Shapes!

Use the information in the shape box to help you uncover the identity of these outlaws. Then draw the shapes on the correct wanted posters. Add faces to the posters if you want to.

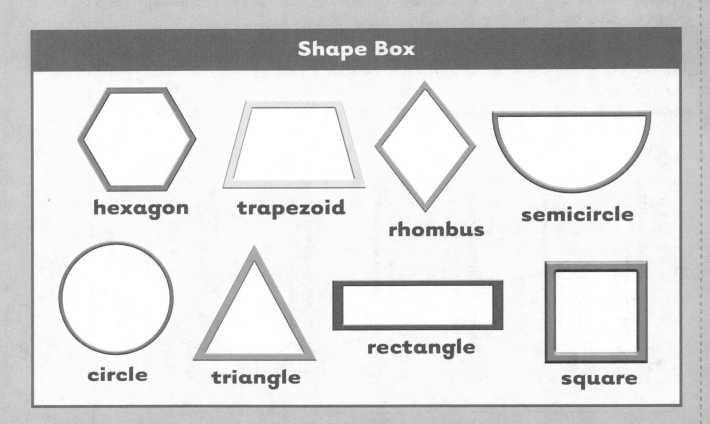

Shape Box

hexagon

trapezoid

rhombus

semicircle

circle

triangle

rectangle

square

Wanted!

1. Description:
Has 4 equal sides and 4 corners

Identity:

_____

Wanted!

2. Description:
Has 6 sides and 6 corners

Identity:

_____

Wanted!

3. Description:
Has 3 sides and 3 corners

Identity:

_____

Wanted!

4. Description:
Has 4 corners and
2 separate pairs
of equal sides

Identity:

_____

Wanted!

5. Description:
Has no straight
lines and no
corners

Identity:

_____

Wanted!

6. Description:
Has 1 flat edge
and 1 curved edge

Identity:

_____

Wanted!

7. Description:
Has 4 equal sides
and 4 corners but
is not a square

Identity:

_____

Wanted!

8. Description:
Has 4 sides and 4
corners. Only 2 of
the sides are equal

Identity:

_____

Shapes! Shapes! Shapes!

Cross out the shape or shapes that do not belong with the shape word.

circle

semicircle

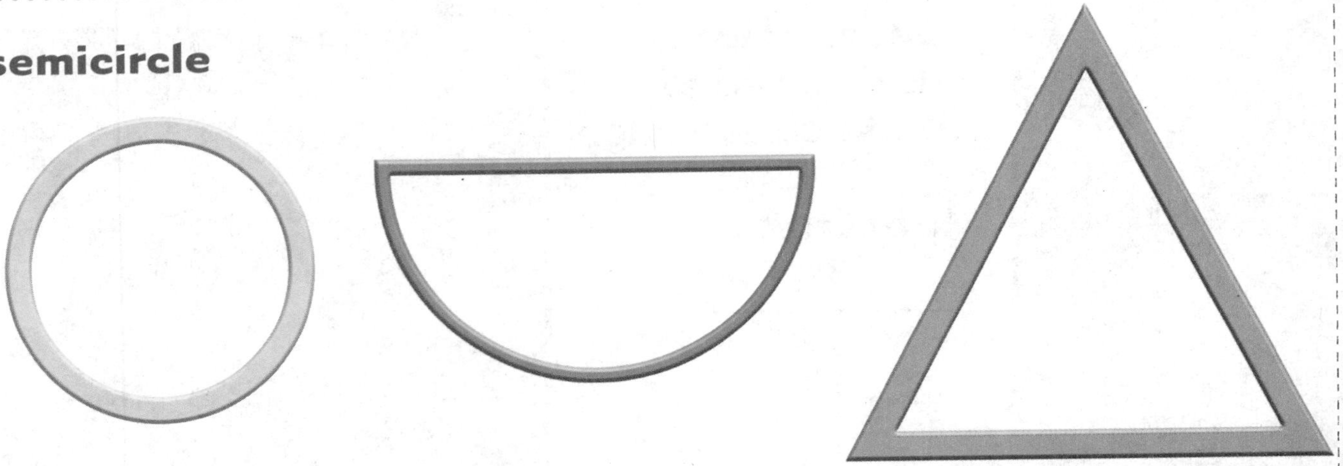

square

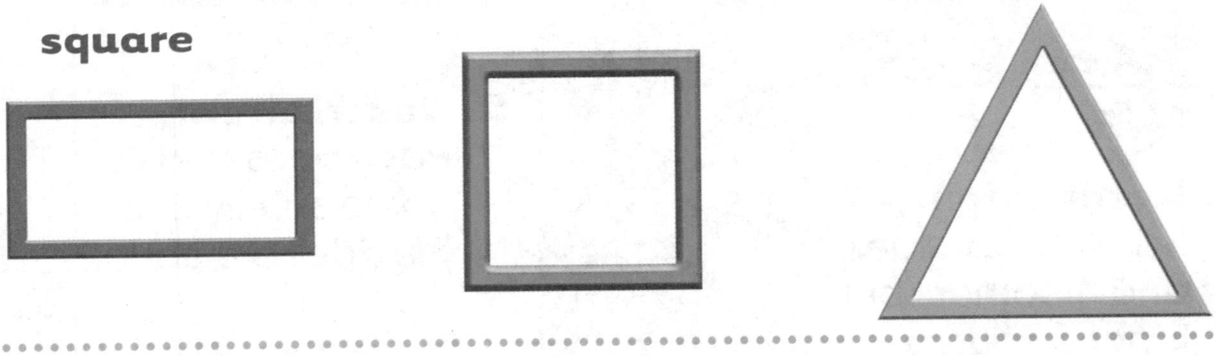

rectangle

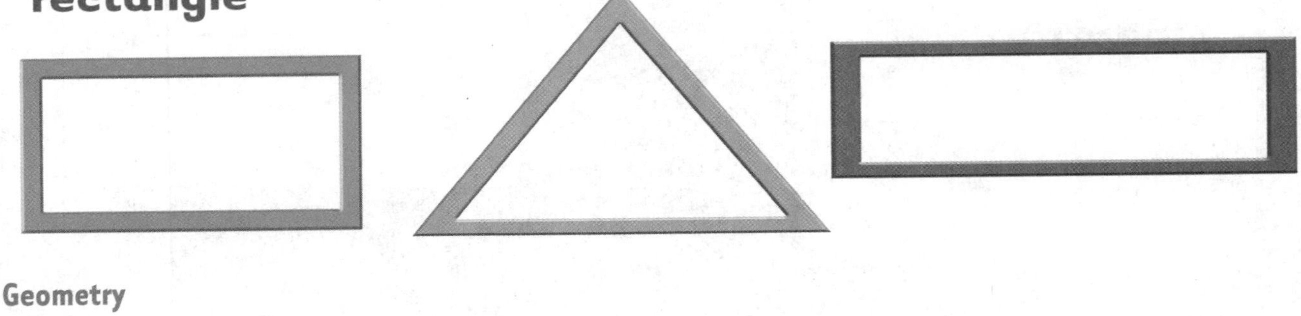

triangle

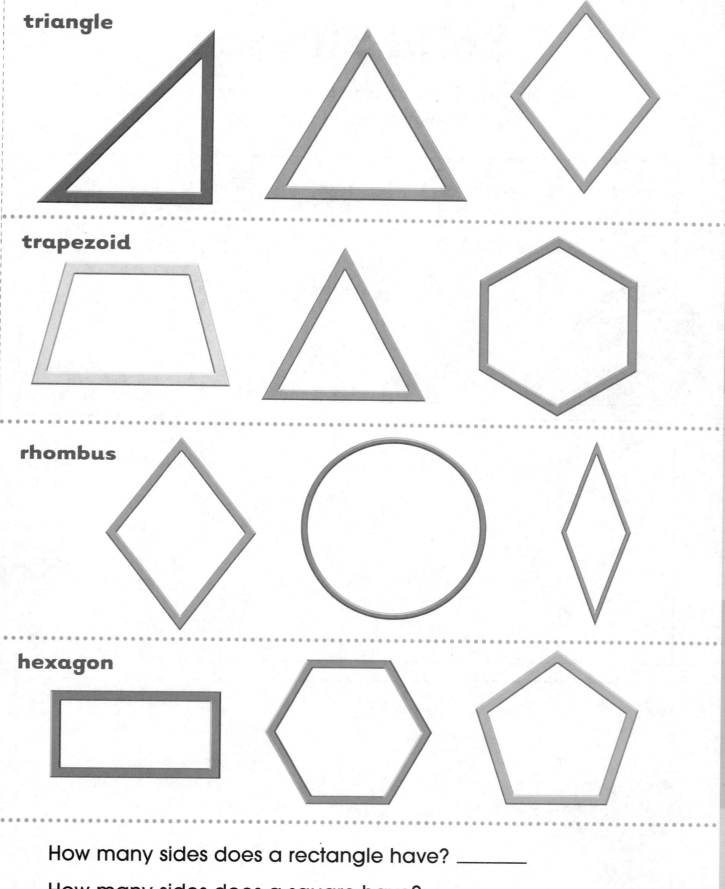

trapezoid

rhombus

hexagon

How many sides does a rectangle have? _____

How many sides does a square have? _____

Which shape has 3 sides? _____

Which shape has 6 sides? _____

Solid Shapes

Draw a picture of something you know that has each of the solid shapes below.

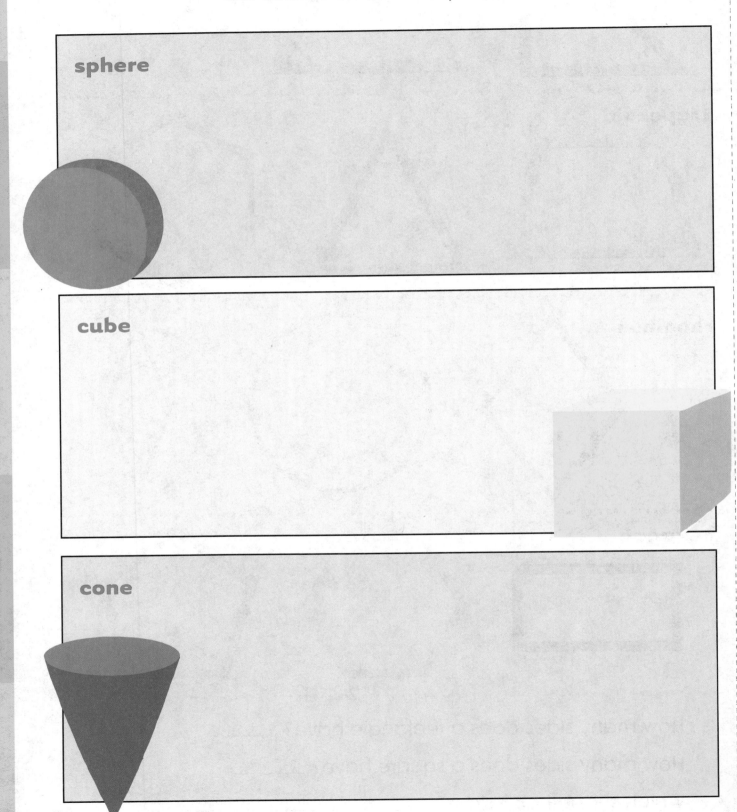

sphere

cube

cone

cylinder

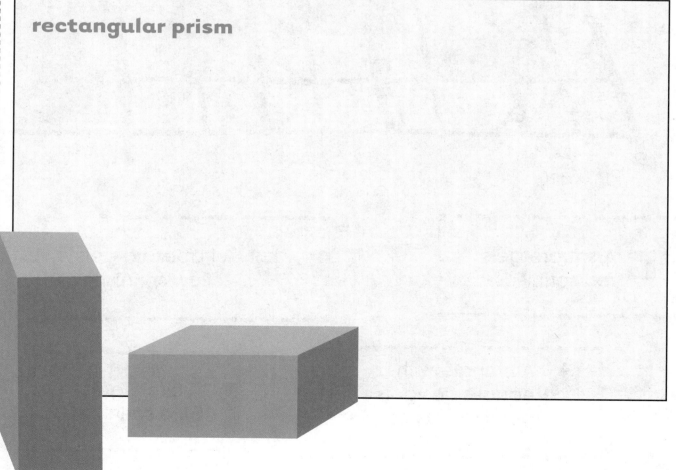

rectangular prism

Yummy Geometry

Use the key below to help you decorate the cookies.

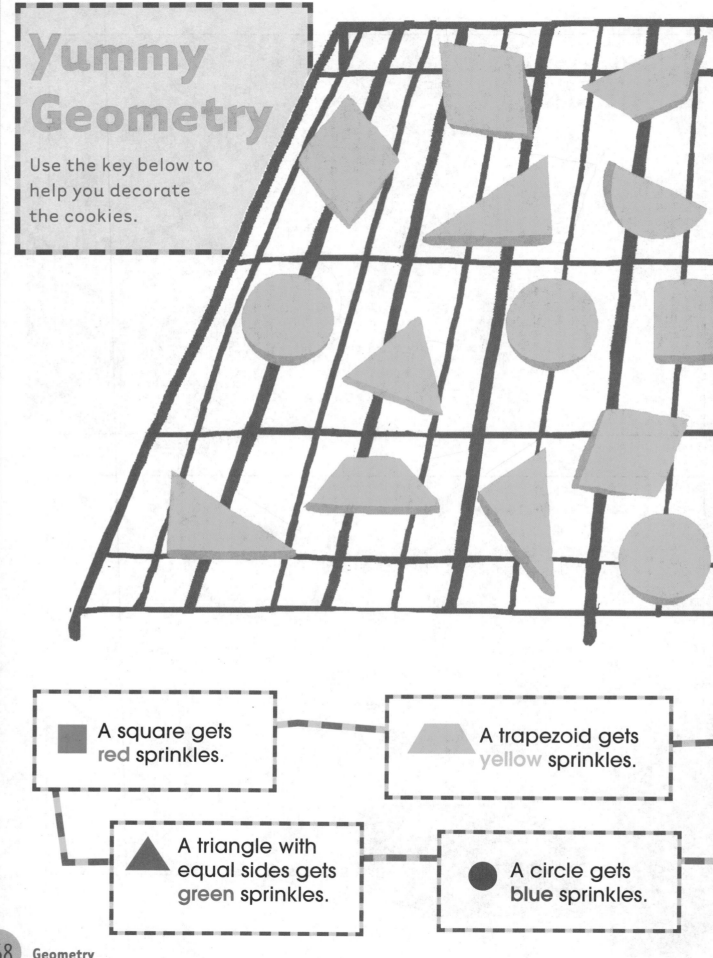

A square gets **red** sprinkles.

A trapezoid gets **yellow** sprinkles.

A triangle with equal sides gets **green** sprinkles.

A circle gets **blue** sprinkles.

 A semicircle get orange sprinkles.

A rhombus gets pink sprinkles.

 A triangle without equal sides gets purple sprinkles.

Combining Shapes

Look at the shapes, and answer the questions.
Fill in the bubble next to the correct answer.

1. Can these shapes be combined to make this circle?

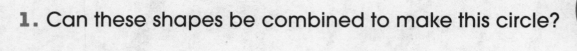

a. ◯ yes   b. ◯ no   c. ◯ yes   d. ◯ no   e. ◯ yes   f. ◯ no

2. Can these shapes be combined to make this square?

c. ◯ yes   d. ◯ no

a. ◯ yes   b. ◯ no   e. ◯ yes   f. ◯ no

3. Can these shapes be combined to make this triangle?

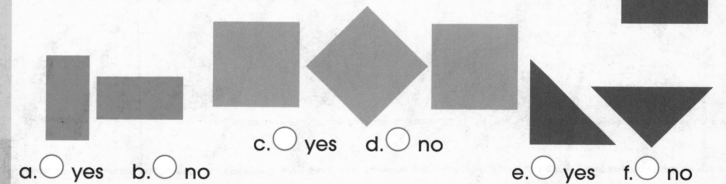

a. ◯ yes   b. ◯ no   c. ◯ yes   d. ◯ no   e. ◯ yes   f. ◯ no

4. Can these shapes be combined to make this rectangle?

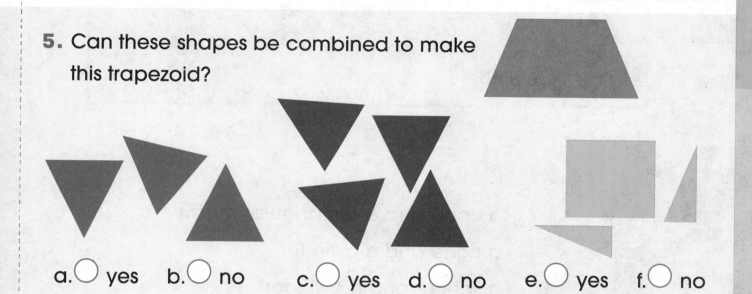

a. ◯ yes   b. ◯ no   c. ◯ yes   d. ◯ no   e. ◯ yes   f. ◯ no

5. Can these shapes be combined to make this trapezoid?

a. ◯ yes   b. ◯ no   c. ◯ yes   d. ◯ no   e. ◯ yes   f. ◯ no

6. Can these shapes be combined to make this rectangle?

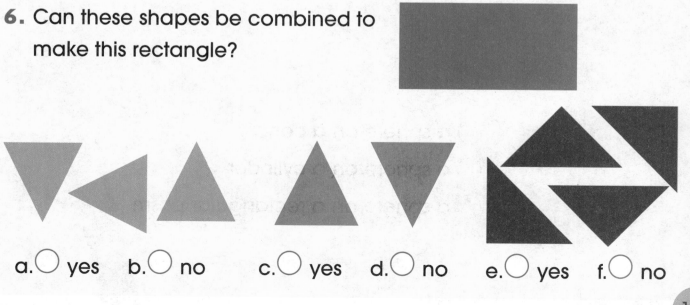

a. ◯ yes   b. ◯ no   c. ◯ yes   d. ◯ no   e. ◯ yes   f. ◯ no

Combine Again

Fill in the bubble next to the answer that best describes each item.

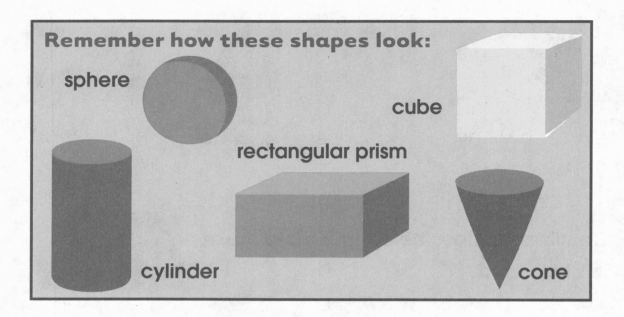

Remember how these shapes look:

sphere

cube

rectangular prism

cylinder

cone

○ a cone and a rectangular prism
○ a cone and a cylinder
○ a sphere and a cylinder

○ a sphere on a cone
○ a sphere on a cylinder
○ a sphere on a rectangular prism

○ 3 rectangular prisms
○ 3 cubes
○ 3 cylinders

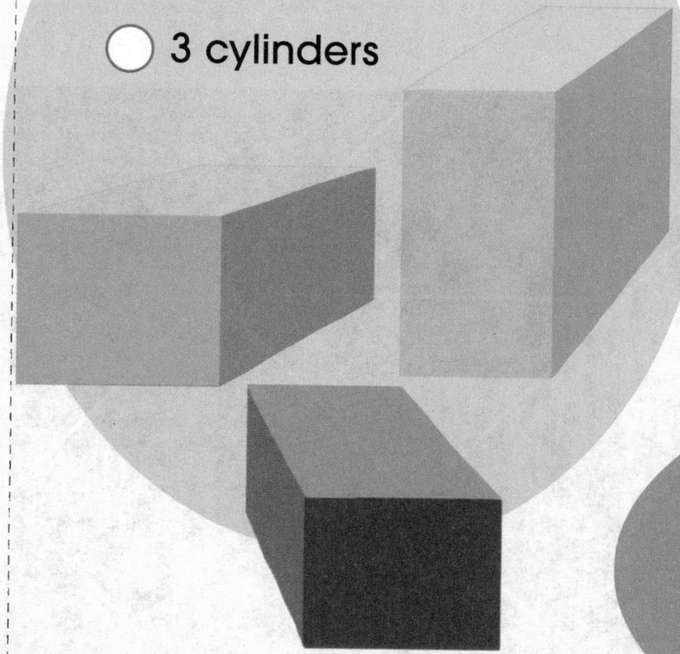

○ a cylinder on a cone
○ a cube on a cylinder
○ a sphere on a cone

○ 3 cubes
○ 3 cones
○ 3 spheres

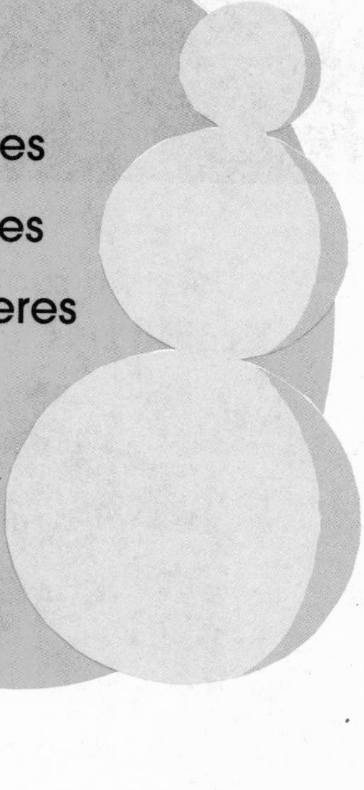

○ 3 spheres
○ 3 cylinders
○ 3 cones

Tangrams

A tangram is a puzzle that uses 7 shapes cut from a square. You can combine the tangram shapes into other shapes and make pictures.

Trace this tangram. Color each piece a different color. Then cut out the pieces. Use the pieces to try the challenges below.

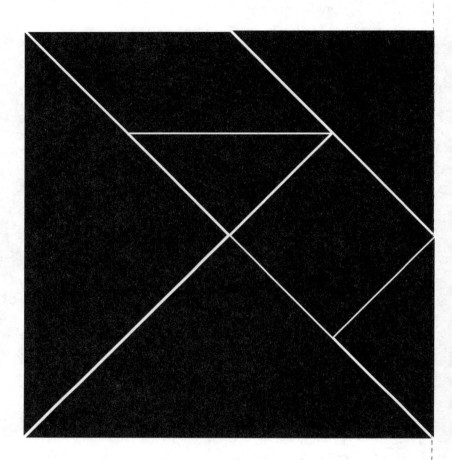

1. Use two tangram pieces to fill this square.

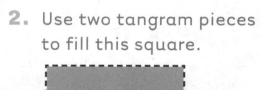

2. Use two tangram pieces to fill this square.

3. Use three tangram
pieces to fill this square.

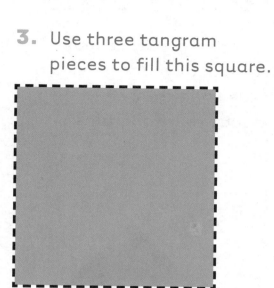

4. Use four tangram pieces
to fill this square.

5. Find a different way to use four
tangram pieces to fill this square.
(Hint: Three are the same, and one
is different.)

More Tangrams

Use all 7 of your tangram pieces to make these figures. Give each of your figures a name. Write it on the line. Now tell someone a story about your tangrams.

_____

_____

_____

Make your own tangram picture here.

Guess My Shape

You'll need a partner, paper, and pencil.

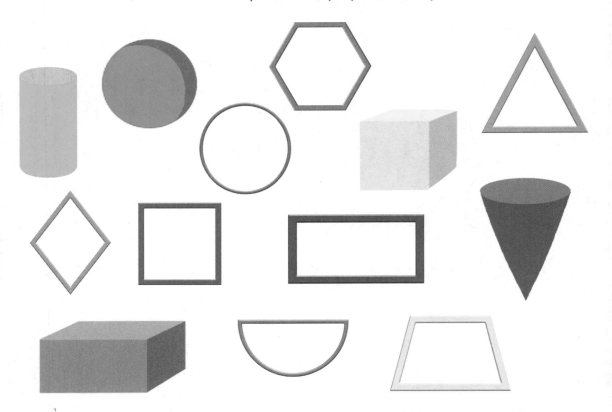

1. Pick one of the shapes on this page. Don't tell your partner which one it is.

2. Have your partner guess which shape you picked. He or she should ask questions about your shape, but only questions that have yes or no answers. Every question is worth 1 point. If your partner thinks he or she knows the shape, then he or she should ask, "Is your shape a . . . ?" If the guess is correct, it's your partner's turn. If not, your partner must keep guessing. Keep track of how many questions are asked.

3. Take turns until you've each had 5 turns.

4. Add up the number of questions each of you has asked. The player with the lowest score wins.

Geometry Answer Key

162–163 1. square or rhombus, 2. hexagon, 3. triangle, 4. rectangle, 5. circle, 6. semicircle, 7. rhombus, 8. trapezoid

164–165 See below; 4, 4, a triangle, a hexagon

166–167 Answers will vary.

168–169 See below.

170–171 1. a, d, e, 2. a, d, e, 3. b, d, f, 4. b, d, f, 5. a, d, f, 6. b, c, f

172–173 a cone and a cylinder, a sphere on a cylinder, 3 rectangular prisms, a sphere on a cone, 3 spheres, 3 cylinders

174–175 See below.

176–177 Tangram names, stories, and pictures will vary.

164–165

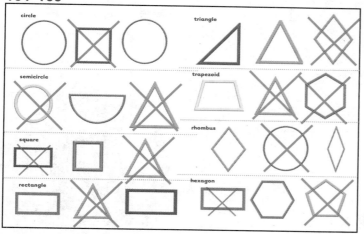

168–169

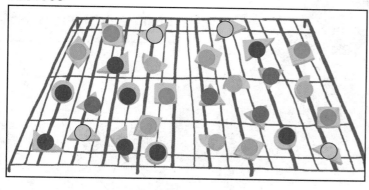

174–175

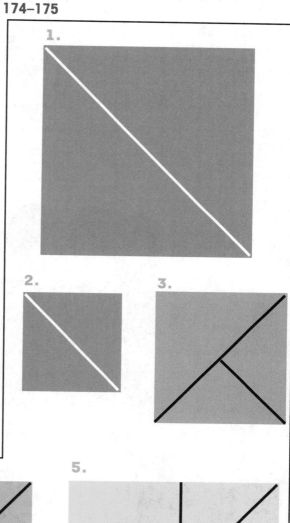

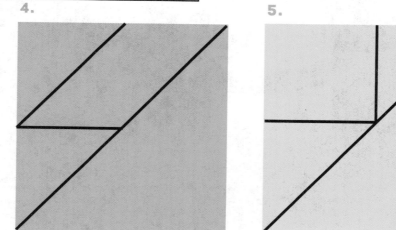

Money, Money, Money!

one penny = 1¢

one nickel = 5¢

one dime = 10¢

one quarter = 25¢

Count the coins in each group.
Write the amount of money
they equal. (Hint: Skip
counting may help you!)

= _____ cents

= _____ cents

= _____ cents

= _____ cents

= _____ cents

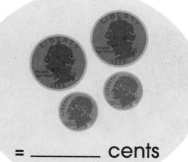

= _____ cents

= _____ cents

= _____ cents

= _____ cents

= _____ cents

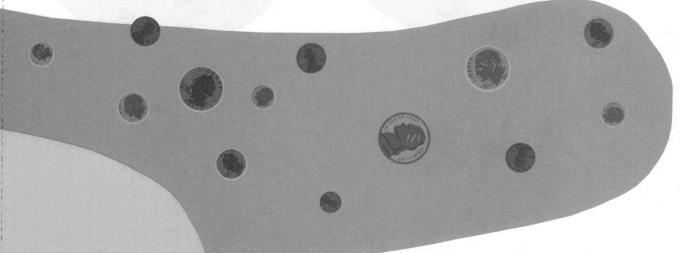

What's It Worth?

Draw lines to match the groups of coins that are worth the same amount. The first one has been done for you.

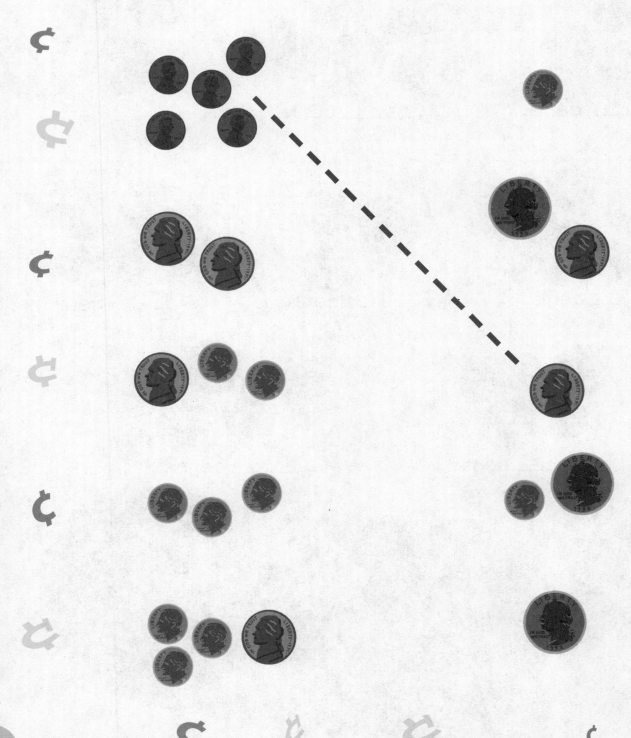

Draw lines to match the groups
of coins with their number values.

   7¢

   15¢

   30¢

   38¢

   60¢

Buying Power

Circle the coins you would need to buy each yard-sale item.

Money in Decimals

This is how you write **one quarter**, or **25¢**, using decimals: **$.25**

Fill in the bubble next to the answer that is the total value of each set of coins.

1.

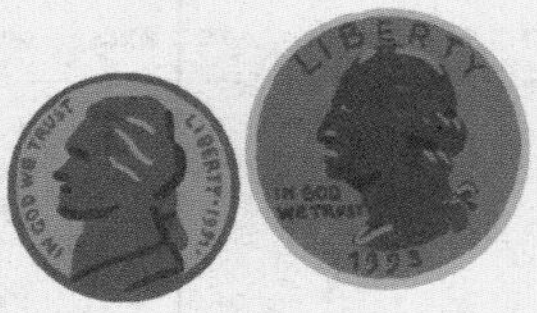

t ◯ $30.00

m ◯ $3.00

r ◯ $.30

2.

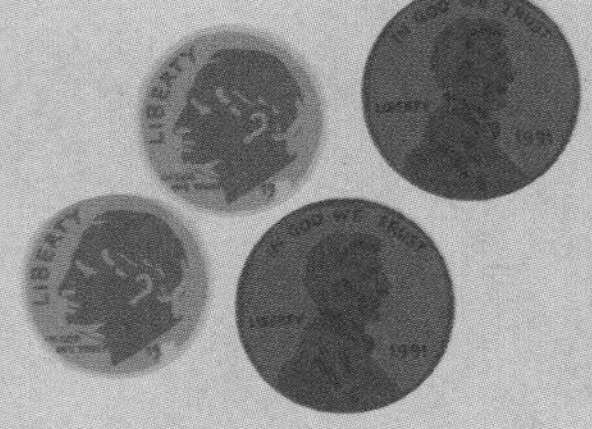

o ◯ $22.22

i ◯ $22.00

e ◯ $.22

3.

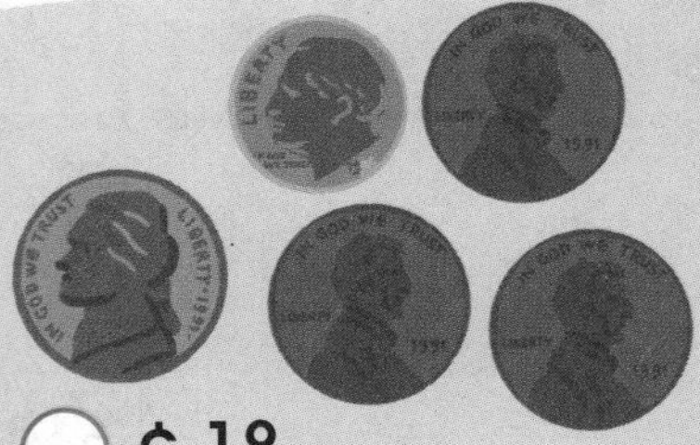

u ◯ ¢.18

a ◯ $.18¢

o ◯ $.18

4.

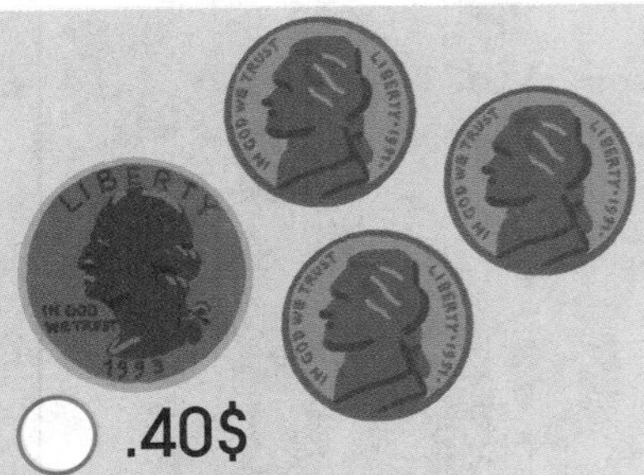

p ◯ .40$

t ◯ $.40

l ◯ .40¢

5.

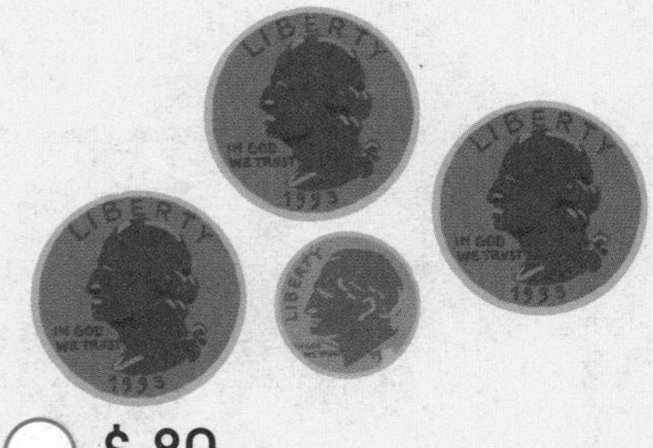

t ◯ $.80

e ◯ $.85

n ◯ $.90

6.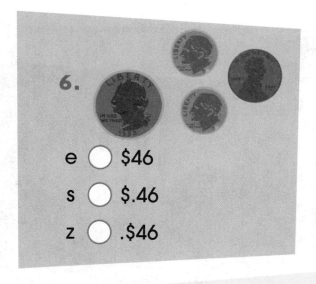

e ◯ $46

s ◯ $.46

z ◯ .$46

7.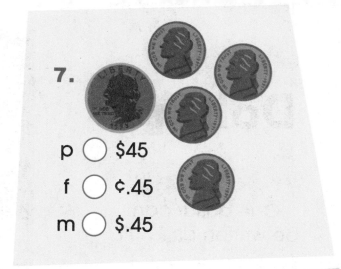

p ◯ $45

f ◯ ¢.45

m ◯ $.45

8.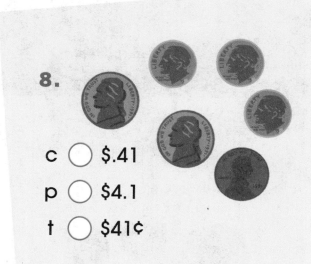

c ◯ $.41

p ◯ $4.1

t ◯ $41¢

9.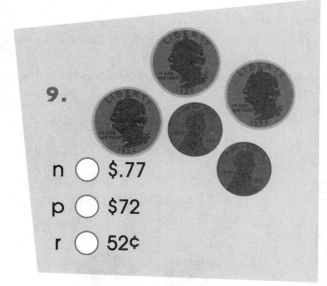

n ◯ $.77

p ◯ $72

r ◯ 52¢

Find the item number that matches each number below. Write the letters next to the answers on the lines below to solve this riddle.

A nickel and a dime walked over a bridge. The nickel climbed onto the railing and fell into the water. Why didn't the dime act like the nickel?

Because the dime had

___ ___ ___ ___
7   3   1   5

___ ___ ___ ___ ___.
8   2   9   4   6

Dollars

One dollar can be written as $1.00.

Circle each group of coins that equals $1.00. Adding or skip counting will help you figure this out.

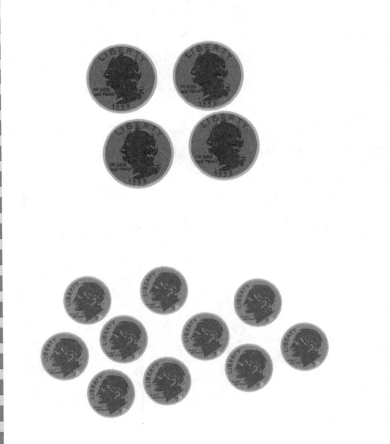

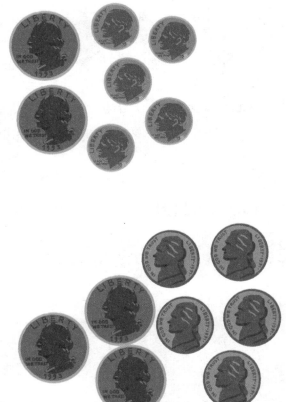

Which group would give you the greater allowance?

Put a ✔ next to it.

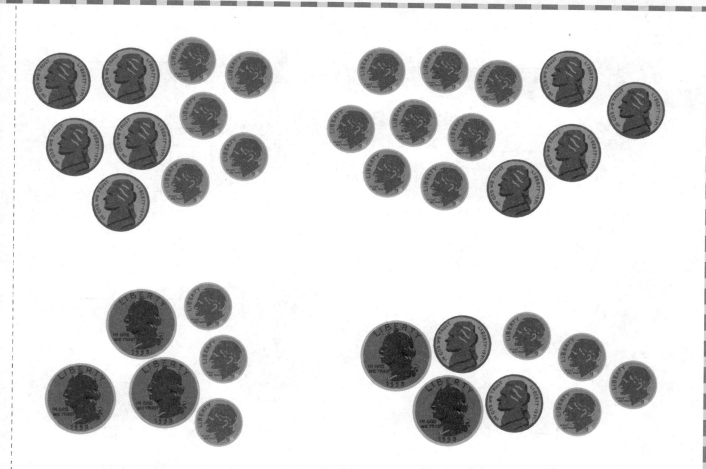

Money Adds Up

Before you add money,
line up the decimal points.

$$\begin{array}{r} \$1.00 \\ +.10 \\ \hline \$1.10 \end{array}$$

Hint: If you have less than 10¢, add a
zero after the decimal point: 9¢ = $.09.

Write a number equation. Then add to get the money amount.

$\underline{}$. $\underline{}$

+ $\underline{}$. $\underline{}$

$\underline{}$. $\underline{}$

$\underline{}$. $\underline{}$

+ $\underline{}$. $\underline{}$

$\underline{}$. $\underline{}$

$\underline{}$. $\underline{}$

+ $\underline{}$. $\underline{}$

$\underline{}$. $\underline{}$

$\underline{}$. $\underline{}$

+ $\underline{}$. $\underline{}$

$\underline{}$. $\underline{}$

$ _____ . _____

_____ . _____

+ _____ . _____
_____

$ _____ . _____

$ _____ . _____

_____ . _____

+ _____ . _____
_____

$ _____ . _____

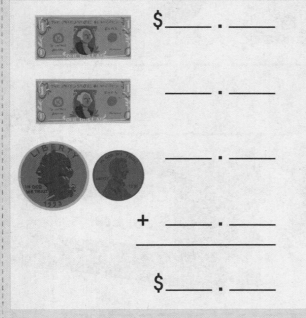

$ _____ . _____

_____ . _____

_____ . _____

+ _____ . _____
_____

$ _____ . _____

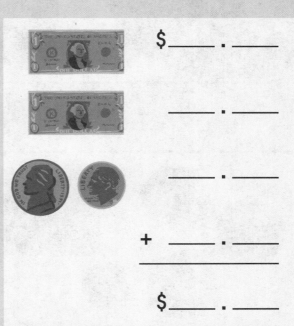

$ _____ . _____

_____ . _____

_____ . _____

+ _____ . _____
_____

$ _____ . _____

Spooky Money

Circle the coins and bills you need to buy each spooky item.

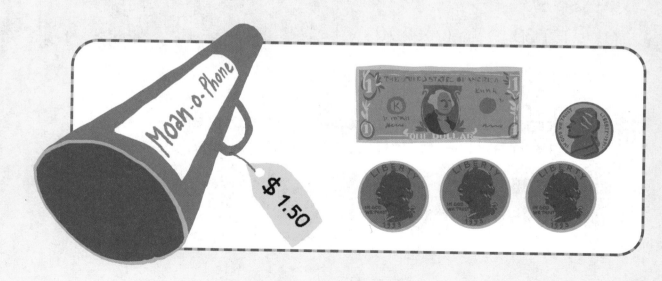

Subtracting Money Values

Before you subtract money values,
line up the decimal points.
You may also have to regroup.

$$\begin{array}{r} \$\overset{0}{\cancel{1}}.\overset{1}{0}0 \\ -.10 \\ \hline \$0.90 \end{array}$$

Fill in the bubbles next to the correct answers to these word problems.

1. Anna has this much money. She gives her brother $1.35. How much does she have now?

   o ◯ $.40   u ◯ $.40

   i ◯ $1.40   a ◯ $1.45

2. Jason has this much money. How much more does he need before he reaches his savings goal of $5.00?

   d ◯ $.30   r ◯ $3.70

   e ◯ $1.30   p ◯ $8.70

3. Ben had $4.70, but he dropped two quarters and a dime. How much does he have left?

   a ◯ $4.35   o ◯ $4.10

   e ◯ $3.60   i ◯ $3.20

4. Mariah had $5.00, but she spent $2.50. How much does she have left?

g ◯ $2.50   m ◯ $2.80

r ◯ $3.30   d ◯ $7.70

5. Chris has $7.80. If he uses this bill and these coins to buy a goldfish, how much money will he have left?

d ◯ $1.50   r ◯ $5.50

b ◯ $6.50   f ◯ $9.10

6. Carlos has this much change in his pocket. After he pays for a bag of chips, he has a quarter, two dimes, and a nickel in his pocket. How much did the chips cost?

p ◯ $.60   h ◯ $.85

r ◯ $.90   t ◯ $.95

7. Jennifer had $5.00. She spent $4.70. How much change did she get?

p ◯ two dimes and a nickel   n ◯ a dollar, a quarter, and a nickel

l ◯ a quarter and a nickel   m ◯ a quarter, a nickel, and a penny

Find the item number that matches each number below. Write the letters next to your answers on the lines below to solve this riddle.

If you put this in your pocket, you'll lose everything. What is it?

A ___ ___ ___
　5　　1　　4

___ ___ ___ ___
6　　3　　7　　2

Same Time, Different Face

One **hour** is made up of 60 minutes. The short hand tells you the hour.

One **half hour** equals 30 minutes.

The long hand on the 6 tells you the half hour.

Some clocks use **00** for the hour and **:30** for the half hour.

Draw lines between the clocks that show the same time.

What is your favorite time?
Draw a clock that shows it.
Write a sentence that tells why.

Give Me Five!

You can use skip counting to tell time. It takes 5 minutes for the minute hand (the long one) to move from number to number on the clock face. Start at the 12 and count by 5s. This clock shows it is 3:05. That means it is five minutes past three o'clock.

Look at this clock.

Where is the minute hand? _____

Count by 5s from the 12 to there: _____

This clock shows 4:15, or a quarter hour. A quarter is the same as $\frac{1}{4}$, and 15 minutes is $\frac{1}{4}$ of the 60 minutes in an hour.

Write the time shown on each clock.

_____

3:15

_____

8:15

_____

_____

_____

_____

Now draw the hands or
write the time on each clock.

8:20

two-thirty

10:15

seven forty-five

quarter past nine

3:15

Circle all the clocks in this activity that show the quarter hour.
(Don't count the example clock.)

How many clocks did you circle? _____

15 minutes = $\frac{1}{4}$ hour

30 minutes = $\frac{1}{2}$ hour

45 minutes = $\frac{3}{4}$ hour

Time Me!

Help Jan the Sports Fan get through her day. Draw clock hands, or write in the time.

Jan wakes up at eight o'clock.

She spends 1 hour eating breakfast and getting dressed in her favorite sports jersey. What time is it now?

She spends 2 hours in the gym. What time is it now?

Jan writes fan letters to her favorite players for 2 hours. What time is it now?

Jan's friend Mike comes for lunch. They eat and trade baseball cards for a half hour. What time is it now?

Jan daydreams about playing professional basketball for another half hour. What time is it now?

Then Jan spends a quarter hour reading a sports magazine. What time is it now?

She spends three-quarters of an hour watching golf on TV. What time is it now?

Jan will eat dinner at 6:00. How many hours is it until she eats? _____

Jan spends 1 hour eating dinner. What time is it now? _____

Jan goes to bed at 9:00. How much time does she have until then? _____

She spends $1\frac{1}{2}$ hours on-line E-mailing friends about sports. How much time does she have left? _____

She spends another quarter hour listening to the radio for the baseball scores. How much time does she have left? _____

She spends a quarter hour brushing her teeth and getting into her sports pajamas. How much time does she have left? _____

Lights out!

Different Time

1. How many seconds are in a minute?

e ◯ 10 r ◯ 30

s ◯ 60 m ◯ 100

2. How many minutes are in an hour?

i ◯ 10 e ◯ 30

o ◯ 60 a ◯ 100

3. How many hours are in a day? Hint: It's more than 10, less than 25, and doesn't have a 0.

t ◯ 12 r ◯ 20

y ◯ 24 y ◯ 30

4. How many days are in a week?

i ◯ 5 n ◯ 6

t ◯ 7 p ◯ 8

5. How many weeks are in a month?

r ◯ about 2 k ◯ 12

h ◯ about 4 l ◯ 52

6. How many months are in a year? Hint: Say the months aloud to yourself, and count.

c ◯ 10 l ◯ 12

s ◯ 52 p ◯ 100

7. Which of these takes about a second? Hint: Get a clock or a watch with a second hand, and try it.

r ◯ clapping once

t ◯ clapping 4 times very fast

p ◯ clapping 40 times very fast

l ◯ clapping 100 times very fast

8. Which of these takes about a minute? (Try it.)

l ◯ singing 1 very fast verse of "Row, Row, Row, Your Boat"

t ◯ singing 10 very fast verses of "Row, Row, Row, Your Boat"

a ◯ singing 100 very fast verses of "Row, Row, Row, Your Boat"

9. Which of these takes about a quarter hour?

m ◯ writing your name

u ◯ writing a 1-page story

d ◯ writing an entire chapter of a book

10. Which of these takes about a half hour?

r ◯ watching a short TV program

s ◯ watching a movie

b ◯ watching 2 movies

11. How long do you sleep at night?

c ◯ about 2 hours

t ◯ about 10 hours

s ◯ about 24 hours

12. How long is your summer vacation?

n ◯ about 2 days

h ◯ about 2 months

k ◯ about 6 months

Find the item number that matches each number below. Write the letters next to your answers on the lines below to solve the riddle.

What time is it when you need a cavity filled?

_____ _____ , _____
  6   4   1

_____ _____ _____ _____ _____ _
  11   2   2   7   5

_____ _____ _____ _____ _____ !
  12   9   10   8   3

Money Game

You'll need a partner, a spinner, a pencil, and a paper clip.

1. Make a spinner (see the picture on page 120). The younger player goes first. Spin. You will get a quarter, dime, nickel, or penny.

2. Look at your scorecard below. Cross out five of the same coins that add up to a multiple of 10. (A multiple of 10 is a number like 20 or 50, but not 35 or 14.) One of the coins must be the same as the one you got on the spinner. Write the sum of your coins on the scorecard.

3. If you can't make a multiple of 10, you still have to cross out 5 coins, but write **0** on your scorecard.

4. Take turns. Play until all of the coins are crossed out. Add up your scores. (You can use a calculator.) The player with the higher score wins.

Name of Player:		Name of Player:	
_____		_____	
1st turn _____		1st turn _____	
2nd turn _____		2nd turn _____	
3rd turn _____		3rd turn _____	
4th turn _____		4th turn _____	
5th turn _____		5th turn _____	
6th turn _____		6th turn _____	
7th turn _____		7th turn _____	
8th turn _____	Total: _____	8th turn _____	Total: _____

Time & Money Answer Key

180–181 30, 20, 25, 26, 75, 70, 35, 33, 51, 96

182–183 See below.

184–185 **Circle** dime, dime, nickel; dime, penny, penny, penny; dime, nickel, penny; quarter, dime, dime, nickel; quarter, dime, nickel, nickel; quarter, quarter dime, nickel, nickel

186–187 1. r, 2. e, 3. o, 4. t, 5. e, 6. s, 7. m, 8. c, 9. n; more cents

188–189 Circle all except the groups of 5 dimes and 5 nickels, 3 quarters and 3 dimes; check the dollar bill, 5 dimes, and 1 nickel

190–191 $.10 + $.01 = $.11, $.10 + $.05 = $.15, $.25 + $.10 = $.35, $1.00 + $.25 = $1.25, $1.00 + $1.00 + $.05 = $2.05, $1.00 + $.25 + $.10 = $1.35, $1.00 + $1.00 + $.25 + $.01 = $2.26, $1.00 + $1.00 + $.05 + $.10 = $2.15

192–193 **Circle** dollar, dollar, dime; dollar, quarter, quarter, dime; dollar, dollar, quarter, quarter, quarter, nickel; dollar, dime, dime, nickel; dollar, dollar, quarter, quarter, quarter; dollar, quarter, quarter

194–195 1. i, 2. e, 3. o, 4. g, 5. b, 6. h, 7. l; big hole

196–197 Draw lines as directed; answers will vary.

198–199 It is on the 3; 5, 10, 15; 7:00, 3:15, 8:15, 9:10, 12:25, 1:25; fill in clocks as directed; 5

200–201 8:00, 9:00, 11:00, 1:00, 1:30, 2:00, 2:15, 3:00, 3, 7:00, 2 hours, one half hour, a quarter-hour, no time

202–203 1. s, 2. o, 3. y, 4. t, 5. h, 6. l, 7. t, 8. t, 9. u, 10. r, 11. t, 12. h; It's tooth-hurty

182–183

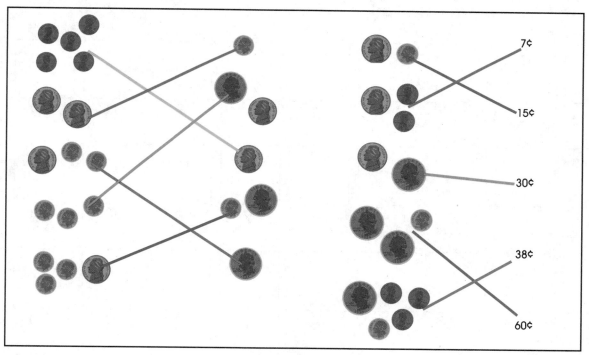

Doggy Graphs!

A **graph** is a way to show information about numbers. Count the brown dogs in each group. Color in the boxes to show how many brown dogs there are. You'll make a graph!

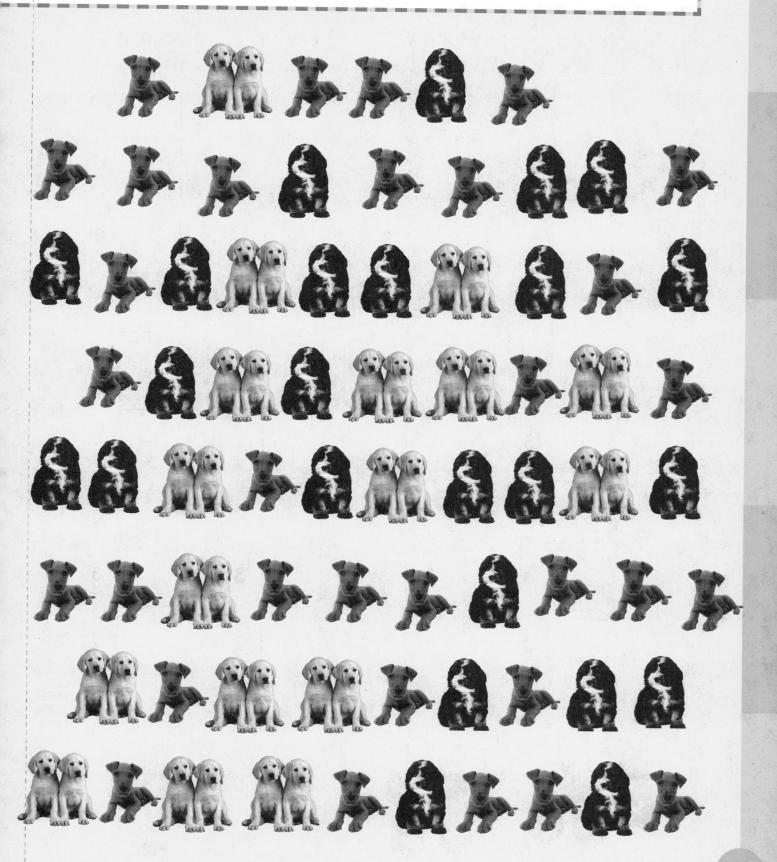

An Apple a Day

Sunday	Monday	Tuesday	Wednesday
☐ 10	☐ 10	☐ 10	☐ 10
☐ 9	☐ 9	☐ 9	☐ 9
☐ 8	☐ 8	☐ 8	☐ 8
☐ 7	☐ 7	☐ 7	☐ 7
☐ 6	☐ 6	☐ 6	☐ 6
☐ 5	☐ 5	☐ 5	☐ 5
☐ 4	☐ 4	☐ 4	☐ 4
☐ 3	☐ 3	☐ 3	☐ 3
☐ 2	☐ 2	☐ 2	☐ 2
☐ 1	☐ 1	☐ 1	☐ 1

Maria loves apples! Count the apples in each group. Color in the boxes to show how many apples Maria ate each day. You'll make another kind of graph!

Thursday	Friday	Saturday
☐ 10	☐ 10	☐ 10
☐ 9	☐ 9	☐ 9
☐ 8	☐ 8	☐ 8
☐ 7	☐ 7	☐ 7
☐ 6	☐ 6	☐ 6
☐ 5	☐ 5	☐ 5
☐ 4	☐ 4	☐ 4
☐ 3	☐ 3	☐ 3
☐ 2	☐ 2	☐ 2
☐ 1	☐ 1	☐ 1

On which day did Maria eat the most apples?

_____

On which day did Maria eat the fewest apples?

_____

Monster Graphs

Answer the questions about each graph.

1. How tall is Skeletron? _____

2. How tall is Toothless Titan? _____

3. Which monster is 40 ft. tall? _____

4. Which two monsters are the same height?

   _____ and _____

5. If Frogzilla stood on Toothless Titan's head,

   what height would they reach? _____

10 legs

8 legs

6 legs

4 legs

2 legs

0 legs

Mega Tiger Rabid Rabbit Mighty Fly Arachnoid

1. How many legs does Rabid Rabbit have? _____

2. Which creature has 6 legs? _____

3. Which creature has the greatest number

 of legs? _____

4. Arachnoid bought a boot for each foot. The boots were too

 tight, so he gave them to Mighty Fly. After Mighty Fly put a

 boot on each foot, how many boots were left? _____

5. Which two creatures together have the same number of

 legs as Arachnoid when you add them together?

 _____ and _____

Eat This Graph

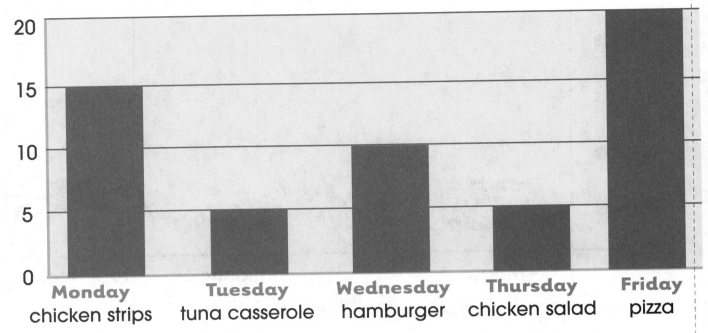

Number of Kids Who Bought School Lunch

Fill in the bubbles next to the answers to these questions about this school-lunch graph.

1. What does this graph show?

t ◯ How many kids bought school lunch on Mondays

g ◯ How many kids bought school lunch each day for a week

f ◯ How many kids bought school lunch each day for a month

n ◯ How many kids like school lunch

2. How many kids bought school lunch on Monday?

n ◯ 20 e ◯ 15

o ◯ 10 l ◯ 5

3. What was served on the day 10 kids bought school lunch?

s ◯ chicken strips

r ◯ tuna casserole

e ◯ hamburger

t ◯ chicken salad

p ◯ pizza

4. What did the school serve on Tuesday?

l ◯ pizza

n ◯ chicken strips

r ◯ tuna casserole

s ◯ chicken salad

5. What lunch did the greatest number of kids buy?

r ◯ hamburger

b ◯ pizza

g ◯ chicken strips

t ◯ tuna casserole

6. On which days did the same number of kids buy a school lunch?

n ◯ Monday and Tuesday

e ◯ Wednesday and Thursday

g ◯ Tuesday and Thursday

l ◯ Thursday and Friday

7. How many kids ate lunch on each of those two days?

l ◯ 20   u ◯ 15

e ◯ 10   o ◯ 5

8. What does the graph tell you?

a ◯ On Monday, 10 kids ate chicken strips.

e ◯ More kids ate hamburger this week than chicken strips.

i ◯ More kids ate pizza this week than tuna casserole.

o ◯ On Wednesday, 20 kids ate hamburger.

9. What do you know is **not** true, according to this graph?

t ◯ This week more kids ate pizza than hamburger.

l ◯ This week more kids ate chicken strips than hamburger.

n ◯ This week more kids ate chicken salad than chicken strips.

Find the item number that matches each number below. Write the letters next to your answers on the lines below to solve the riddle.

One lunch server has 3 piles of canned corn. Another lunch server has 6 piles of canned corn. If they combine them, how many piles of canned corn will they have?

_____ _____ _____, only
  7   9   3

_____ _____ _____ _____ _____ _____!
  5   8   1   6   2   4

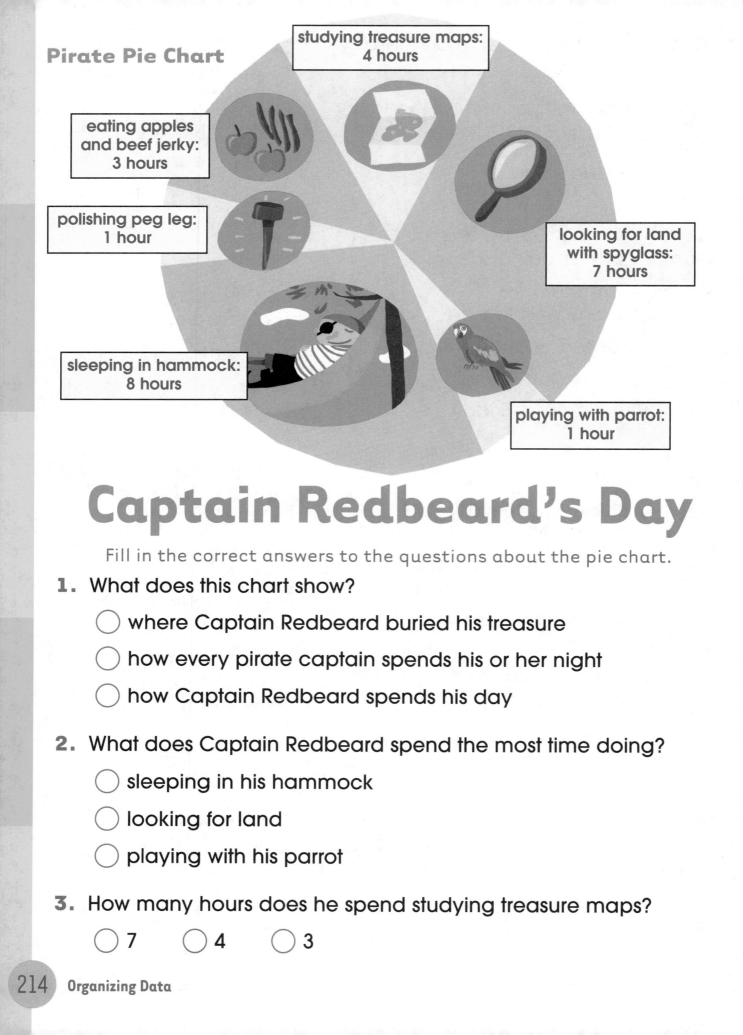

studying treasure maps:
4 hours

eating apples
and beef jerky:
3 hours

polishing peg leg:
1 hour

looking for land
with spyglass:
7 hours

sleeping in hammock:
8 hours

playing with parrot:
1 hour

Captain Redbeard's Day

Fill in the correct answers to the questions about the pie chart.

1. What does this chart show?

○ where Captain Redbeard buried his treasure

○ how every pirate captain spends his or her night

○ how Captain Redbeard spends his day

2. What does Captain Redbeard spend the most time doing?

○ sleeping in his hammock

○ looking for land

○ playing with his parrot

3. How many hours does he spend studying treasure maps?

○ 7   ○ 4   ○ 3

4. What two activities does Captain Redbeard spend the same doing?

○ sleeping and eating

○ playing with his parrot and polishing his peg leg

○ looking for land and studying treasure maps

A **pictograph** is a chart that uses pictures.
You can make one based on the pirate pie chart.

1. Find the first item to be filled in: sleeping. Look at the pirate pie chart. How many hours does Captain Redbeard spend sleeping?

2. Draw a hammock for each hour he spends sleeping. Put each picture on top of the other. You should reach the number 8.

3. Do the same for Captain Redbeard's other activities.

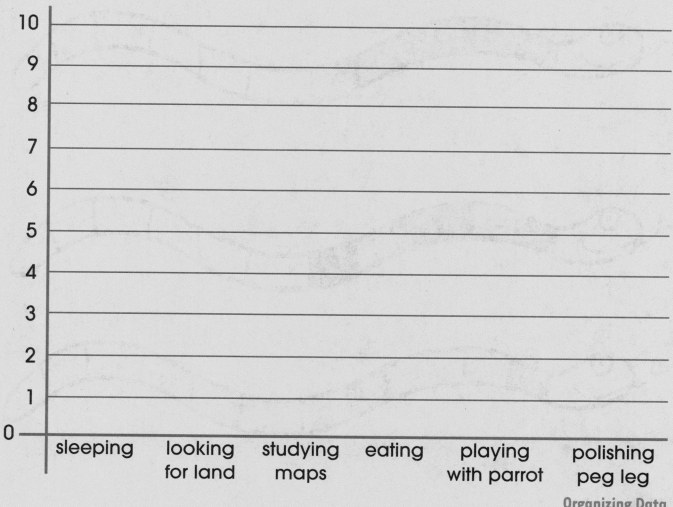

Patternsssss

Look at the colors on each snake.
Color in the rest of each snake to follow the pattern.

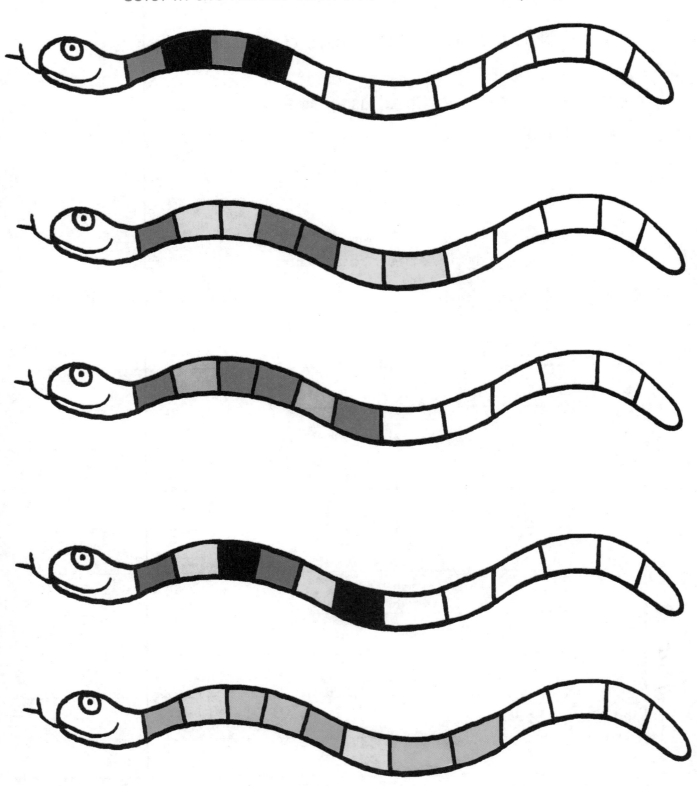

Organizing Data

Now fill in the missing colors based on the pattern.

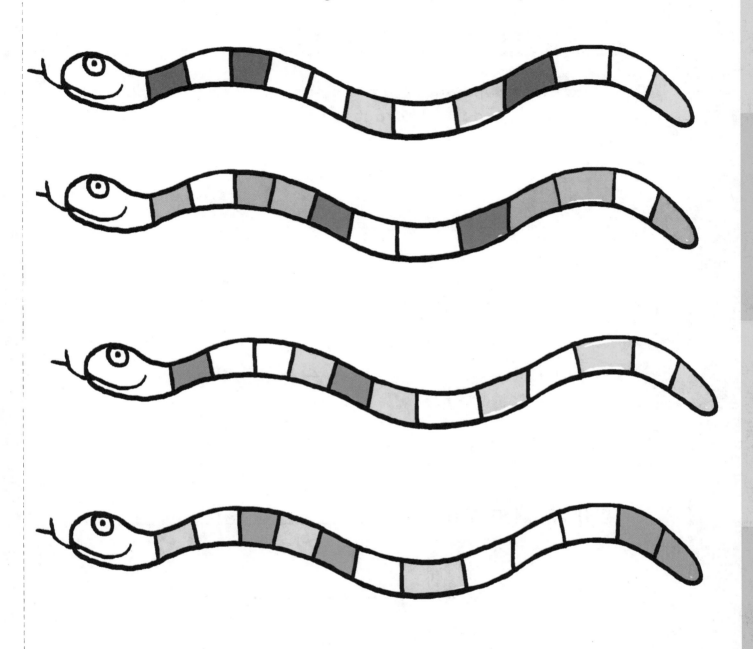

Color your own pattern on this snake.

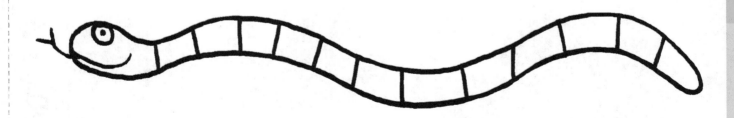

Number Patterns

Continue these number patterns. Hint: Think about the number you would add or subtract to get the next number.

2, 4, 6, _____, _____, _____, _____

10, 11, 12, 13, _____, _____, _____, _____

5, 7, 9, 11, _____, _____, _____, _____

80, 70, 60, 50, _____, _____, _____, _____

250, 350, 450, 550, _____, _____, _____, _____

3, 6, 9, 12, _____, _____, _____, _____

60, 55, 50, 45, _____, _____, _____, _____

Now try these tricky patterns. Hint: You may have to look at three numbers and do two steps to figure out the next number.

2, 3, 5, 6, 8, 9, _____, _____, _____, _____

2, 1, 3, 2, 4, 3, 5, 4, _____, _____, _____, _____

Make up your own number pattern.

_____

Likely or Unlikely?

Aliens have invited you to dinner. Can you figure out what is likely and unlikely to happen during each course? The number of things and amounts in the pictures will give you clues. Write your answers on the lines.

Your alien host will lead you to a seat. How many legs will be on the chair you are **likely** to get? _____

How many legs are on the chair you are **unlikely** to get? _____

The aliens are serving their favorite soup. Are you **likely** to get more eyeballs, more worms, or the same amount of each?

_____

The alien chef will mix these snacks into one big bowl. When guests take a handful, which snack are they **unlikely** to get?

_____

Reach up to the tray for something to drink. Are you likely or unlikely to grab a glass of milk?

_____

Who is likely to finish the soup first: you or the alien sitting next to you?

_____

After dinner, the aliens like to dance. There are 41 aliens and you. Is everyone likely or unlikely to have a partner?

_____

Are you likely or unlikely to go to another alien dinner? _____

Tell why. _____

_____

_____

Repeat After Me

You'll need a partner, pencil, and paper.

Round One

1. One player makes sounds that follow a pattern—for example, "Beep, beep, boop, beep, beep, boop . . ."

2. The other player repeats the same pattern with a different set of sounds—for example, "Fork, fork, knife, fork, fork, knife . . ." The first player decides whether it is the same pattern. If it is, the second player gets a point.

3. Each player takes three turns in each role.

Round Two

1. One player makes sounds that follow a pattern—for example, "Slosh, slosh, slish, slish, slosh, slosh, slish, slish . . ."

2. The other player repeats the pattern with hand and body motions—for example, wave, wave, clap, clap, wave, wave, clap, clap. The first player decides whether the motions follow the same pattern. If they do, the second player gets a point.

3. Each player takes three turns in each role.

Round Three

1. One player makes sounds that follow a pattern—for example, "Nee, nah, nee, nee, nah, nee . . ."

2. The other player draws a line of shapes, letters, or numbers that uses the same pattern—for example, X O X X O X. The first player decides whether the shapes follow the same pattern. If they do, the second player gets a point.

3. Each player takes three turns in each role.

The player with the most points wins. Or just play for fun!

Organizing Data Answer Key

206–207 See below.

208–209 5, 4, 1, 3, 6, 2, 7; Saturday, Tuesday

210–211 1. 30 ft., 2. 50 ft., 3. Frogzilla, 4. Skeletron, Zaniac, 5. 90 ft.; 1. 4, 2. Mighty Fly, 3. Arachnoid, 4. 2, 5. Mega Tiger, Rabid Rabbit

212–213 1. g, 2. e, 3. e, 4. r, 5. b, 6. g, 7. o, 8. i, 9. n; one, bigger

214–215 1. how Captain Redbeard spends his day, 2. sleeping in his hammock, 3. 4, 4. playing with his parrot and polishing his peg leg; draw pictograph as directed.

216–217 See below; patterns will vary.

218–219 8, 10, 12, 14; 14, 15, 16, 17; 13, 15, 17, 19; 40, 30, 20, 10; 650, 750, 850, 950; 15, 18, 21, 24; 40, 35, 30, 25; 11, 12, 14, 15 (add 2, add 1); 6, 5, 7, 6 (add 2, subtract 1); patterns will vary.

220–221 3, 5; more eyeballs; Lx Bits; unlikely; the alien sitting next to you; likely; answers will vary.

206–207

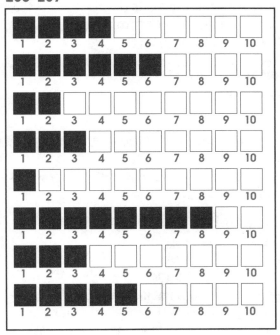

216–217

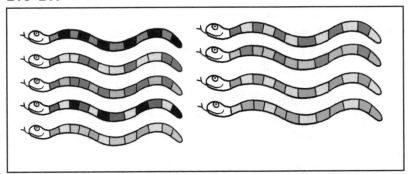

Math Skills

These essential math skills are covered on the following activity pages:

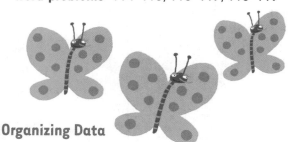